COLOSTRUM

Spiritual Antibodies for New Christians

Rev. David L. Greentree

Colostrum

Spiritual Antibodies for New Christians

Rev. David L. Greentree

ISBN: 978-0-9923561-0-1

All Bible references are from the New International
Version, unless otherwise stated.

Table of Content

Foreword

In this booklet my aim is to give helpful information for new Christians.

In over 30 years of ministry as an ordained Anglican minister, I have had the joy of seeing lots of people - old and young - find new life in Jesus. However, coming to Christ is just the beginning of the journey. I have also had the heartache of seeing many succumb to spiritual "illnesses" and fraudsters so that they lose their way. I have learned the hard way how to protect young believers from these perils.

I make no claim to being a theologian - but I am pretty good at spiritual infant welfare, and an effective spiritual kindergarten teacher!

So what I have done here is to share my very hard won practical experience. I pray you find it helpful.

PART ONE

INTRODUCTION

CHAPTER ONE

The Makings of A Christian

Are You A Christian?

Are you a Christian?

If you don't think you are a Christian, please find someone who can tell you about the Good News of Jesus Christ right away. Your eternal destiny - whether you end up in heaven with God or receive the default choice: hell - is at stake!

If you do think you are a Christian here is a little self-test you can take.

These are the questions which candidates for baptism have to answer. I am using the wording from the 1662 Anglican service here but the gist is pretty universal I think, though I've added notes below.

> Question: DOST thou renounce the devil and all his works, the vain pomp and glory of the world, with all covetous desires of the same, and the carnal desires of the flesh, so that thou wilt not follow, nor be led by them?
> *Answer: I renounce them all.*
> Question: DOST thou believe in God the Father Almighty, Maker of heaven and earth? And in Jesus Christ his only begotten Son our Lord? And that he was conceived by the Holy Ghost; born of the Virgin Mary;

that he suffered under Pontius Pilate, was crucified, dead, and buried; that he went down into hell, and also did rise again the third day; that he ascended into heaven, and sitteth at the right hand of God the Father Almighty; and from thence shall come again at the end of the world, to judge the quick and the dead?

And dost thou believe in the Holy Ghost; the holy Catholick Church; the Communion of Saints; the Remission of sins; the Resurrection of the flesh; and everlasting life after death?

Answer: All this I steadfastly believe.

Question: WILT thou be baptized in this faith?

Answer: That is my desire.

Question: WILT thou then obediently keep God's holy will and commandments, and walk in the same all the days of thy life?

Answer: I will endeavour so to do, God being my helper.

Permit me to make some explanatory remarks.

Question one is basically asking you to change sides in the war of the universe. It assumes you have been on the Devil's turf, at least in the role of a citizen of an occupied country (think maybe of a French person during the Nazi occupation). Now you are being asked to disavow that and take up active allegiance to God instead.

In the world under the rule of the Devil, our lives are largely governed by a false (but very clever and appealing) worldview maintained by the Devil, here called "the vain pomp and glory of the world" and "the covetous desires of the same". This also includes the flawed promptings and yearnings of our human nature called here "the carnal desires of the flesh." We have to decide to turn our back on these illusions and learn to say "No!" to our old human nature if we want to come over to God's side.

Question two is "do you believe what all Christians through all history all over the world have said was their essential belief?" summed up here in what we call the Apostle's Creed.

The phrase "holy Catholick Church" can cause some confusion, so please let me explain: "catholic" just means "universal" and "church" in the New Testament is the Koine Greek word *ekklesia* which means "a gathering, assembly or crowd". So here we are not affirming any denominational church (Roman Catholic or otherwise) but something spine tinglingly wonderful; membership of "God's Crowd" composed not only of people we can see now but of all the people who have ever or will ever belong to Jesus, from every tribe and nation (and every "church") which will have its first full meeting when Jesus returns. That will be some meeting, some party!

Question three involves a declaration of obedience to God.

So what about you? Right here right now. Do you answer all those questions in the affirmative?

If you say "No" then this book is not designed to meet your present needs, but please do feel free to keep reading because it may excite your interest in finding out more about Jesus.

Choosing God

Choosing God takes effort. Choosing God goes against our pride, because we have to admit to ourselves that we can't do it on our own, we need God. Choosing God seems silly whilst we are caught up in the Devil's lies and the worldview he manages to hoodwink most people into believing is reality. Choosing God means committing to a way of life going "against the tide" of what most people think. A way of life that the rest of the world may try to make uncomfortable and sometimes short! Choosing God means committing to a minute by minute, day by day struggle living God's way, not the way of our warped human nature. It is choosing a lifestyle that takes all the power and resources that God provides and at times all our strength and willpower to maintain.

Only after choosing God can we appreciate the benefits. We are now reconciled to God: no longer afraid of his judgement, but as a beloved child being in rapt wonder at his greatness and love. No longer following human religion with its rules and rituals, but having in our innermost being the presence of God the Holy Spirit. No longer afraid of the terrors life can throw up, but knowing that Jesus is standing shoulder to shoulder with us facing them and that the trials of this life will seem nothing compared to the rewards of heaven. No longer living a life either in fear of death or hiding that fear only by myths of immortality, but with the real certainty of resurrection to eternal life in heaven with Christ.

There is a "default" choice: it is not (yet) choosing to take up God's offer on amnesty in Christ. This choice is really easy to make: you don't have to think about it at all. That is why I called it the "default" choice. Most people stick with the default choice. While you stick with it, God will honour your choice and limit his involvement in your life (but he will still be there because he wants you to choose him after all). So you will probably make a series of bad choices in your life with bad consequences for you and others. You will maybe feel a nagging "God shaped hole" in your life which you will try to plug with other things: religion, money, drugs, sex, power and so on.

If you stick with the default choice till you die you will get the eternal consequences of your choice - total exclusion from God, heaven and all the people who chose God while they could, and from everything that is good, lovely and desirable because all these things come from God. What you will be left with, forever, is called "hell".

Your future: your choice!

God's Grace

Re-reading the last section I can see that some of my fellow believers will think I have over-emphasised the "your choice" aspect. They are in theory right. Without the sheer abundance of God's kindness, goodness and love that we call "grace" we would have no choice at all. We are all sinners, the Bible makes that plain. God as judge of the entire world should send every last one of us to hell. God as a being who hates evil with a passion should have nothing to do with us humans who are as covered in evil as kids playing in a mud patch are covered in dirt.

That is part of the wonder of God. We can never plumb the depths of it. He hates sin but he loves us sinners. He went so far as to come to earth, born as a human baby, to deal with sin. Jesus was simultaneously both God and human. In fact, he was THE representative of the human race. When he suffered and died on the cross evil was disarmed.

Theologians down the centuries have tried to make up some illustration for the people of their time to explain this. These illustrations have generally seemed a bit lame to the people of the next generation. So maybe it is safer to say: "It just IS". Or to stick with the words of the Bible, like these;

For God so loved the world that he gave his one and only Son, that whoever believes in him shall not perish but have eternal life. (John 3.16)

Just as the Son of Man did not come to be served, but to serve, and to give his life as a ransom for many. (Matthew 20.28)

For all have sinned and fall short of the glory of God, and all are justified freely by his grace through the redemption that came by Christ Jesus. God presented Christ as a sacrifice of atonement, through the shedding of his blood - to be received by faith. He did this to demonstrate his justice, because in his forbearance he had left the sins committed beforehand unpunished - he did it to demonstrate his justice at the present time, so as to be just and the one who justifies those who have faith in Jesus. (Romans 3.23-26)

This concise statement in Romans is so important that I will paste in the *New Living Translation* version as well:

For everyone has sinned; we all fall short of God's glorious standard. Yet God, with undeserved kindness, declares that we are righteous. He did this through Christ Jesus when he freed us from the penalty for our sins. For God presented Jesus as the sacrifice for sin. People are made right with God when they believe that Jesus sacrificed his life, shedding his blood. This sacrifice shows that God was being fair when he held back and did not punish those who sinned in times past, for he was looking ahead and including them in what he would do in this present time. God did this to demonstrate his righteousness, for he himself is fair and just, and he declares sinners to be right in his sight when they believe in Jesus. (Romans 3:23-26)

He himself bore our sins in his body on the cross,
so that we might die to sins and live for righteousness;
by his wounds you have been healed. (1 Peter 2.24)

That of course is only a tiny selection of Bible
verses, but enough for the present to make the point
that Jesus dying on the cross was essential to God
forgiving our sins.

The really vital news is that Jesus did die for us
and God does forgive us our sins and amazingly adopt
us as his sons and daughters when we turn away from
our old life of rebellion and come back to him.

God's Power and Work

I ended my last section saying that the really vital
news is that Jesus did die for us and God does forgive
us our sins and take us back as beloved sons and
daughters when we turn away from our old way of life
and come back to him. I need to amplify that in one
more respect. The choice is all ours - that is true! The
work is all God's - that is doubly true!

As I said, Jesus died for us and rose again from
the dead. Without that there would be no hope and no
forgiveness. Our 'choice' even if we could make it
would have as little effect as flicking a light switch
after a storm had brought down all the electricity
wires!

There is yet another essential work that is totally
God's. Just as Adam and Eve hid from God after that
first disobedience, after so many generations of
rebellion against God and after so many personal
choices to go against him and all he stands for, we
humans are utterly incapable of doing a turn-around
and choosing God. (The real God I mean - humans
are very good at choosing and serving the 'gods'

created by their own imagination. The very fact that we do invent 'gods' that we feel comfortable with supports the point that we cannot by ourselves face the real one!)

The good news here is that what we could never do, God again accomplishes for us. God really wants to save us, and so gives us ample opportunity to choose. He will not force us to choose him, but he does absolutely everything necessary so that we CAN choose him.

Here is just one more instance of how marvellous beyond description God is. His Holy Spirit works inside us to let us choose. God opens our minds to get a glimmer of his love for us. God plants the seed in our consciousness of the reality that after all we have been and done, the real God, the one we are afraid to think about, will take us back. More than that, he even uses our moments of desperation as a catalyst for us to choose to ask for his help. The biblical image is of the conscientious shepherd searching for his lost sheep, finding it, and when it is too exhausted to do anything, carrying it home on his shoulder.

So at the judgement we who chose God will know we did nothing to merit the joys of heaven which are before us. At the same time those who did not choose God will know with dread certainty that God made so many perfect opportunities for them to choose him that they are totally responsible for the awful fate that awaits them.

Let me say it again. God has done, does do, will do everything to save us - everything EXCEPT force us. He made us with free will and will not take it away from us. Of course he could, he just won't. He wants us to choose to love him.

So the bottom line is that what I said about us having a choice is true. But I did need to add that we only have that choice because God has done everything else necessary. The fact that God has done all this to give us that choice leaves us totally without excuse if we don't use it. As the Bible says in Hebrews 2.3 "how shall we escape if we ignore so great a salvation?"

CHAPTER TWO

Being Reborn

Spiritual Babies

Back to the "do you here and now say 'yes' to the baptism questions?"

If you "generally" believe but have issues, read on: you might just have been brought down by a spiritual virus. Also, a book like C.S. Lewis' *Mere Christianity* explains Christian certainties much better than I can, so may help as well.

If you say "yes" then you are a child of God. You have been born again. Your sins have been forgiven. You have been delivered from the dominion of darkness into the kingdom of Jesus, God's dear son. You have been born again into a living hope by the resurrection of Jesus Christ from the dead: the sure and certain hope of resurrection from the dead and sharing Christ's glory in heaven.

If this is a recent decision, then you are, spiritually speaking, a new-born baby in your faith in Jesus. On the other hand, this may have happened sometime ago and you may now be on your journey growing to maturity in Christ. You may even be nearing the end of your travels with Christ in this life and be ready to say with Paul and countless others, "I have fought the good fight, I have finished the race, I have kept the faith. Now there is in store for me the crown of righteousness, which the Lord, the righteous Judge, will award to me on that day - and not only to me, but also to all who have longed for his appearing." (2 Timothy 4.7,8).

This book is aimed at people in the first category: spiritual babies. Peter in his first letter says to his readers, "Like newborn babies, crave pure spiritual milk, so that by it you may grow up in your salvation." But in the case of physical babies, the first thing they receive after their time growing in the womb is not milk but a fluid called "colostrum". Once they are born they are at risk of attack from bacteria and viruses. The first thing they receive from their mother's breast, even before the nourishing milk they will need, is a fluid containing antibodies manufactured by their mother's immune system. These antibodies will give them initial disease protection until their own immune system has become practised at making its own antibodies in response to virus attack.

Just as physical babies are at risk from all the viruses floating around, so spiritual babies are at risk from virus-like false teaching. New born Christians need spiritual colostrum from the start. As James said in his letter:

> Dear friends, although I was very eager to write to you about the salvation we share, I felt compelled to write and urge you to contend for the faith that was once for all entrusted to God's holy people. For certain individuals whose condemnation was written about long ago have secretly slipped in among you. They are ungodly people, who pervert the grace of our God into a license for immorality and deny Jesus Christ our only Sovereign and Lord.

This book is intended to be spiritual colostrum, immunising new Christians against the most common "viruses" until they have grown in their understanding of the Bible and their relationship with Jesus so that they can pick false and deceptive teachings for themselves.

Why You Need Antibodies

You might as well ask why we need antibodies in a physical sense. The answer is simple: that is just the way the world is. From the moment we are born there are viruses all around us that will attack our bodies. Without an immune reaction we would die.

You might as well ask why we install anti-virus software on our computers. The answer is that there just are humans out there devising virus like programs to attack our computers.

As you read the pages of the Old Testament you will see that God's people were continually being led astray by false teachers, importing bits from pagan religions and ending up deserting the real God altogether. When you come to the New Testament, Paul's letters make it plain that almost as soon as he had travelled through a region bringing people to faith in Jesus, false teachers moved in and started destroying the faith of these new believers.

Even after all the time Paul spent back and forth visiting the Christian community at Ephesus, as he said good-bye to them knowing that he would probably be imprisoned and never see them again, he warned:

> I know that after I leave, savage wolves will come in among you and will not spare the flock. Even from

your own number some will arise and distort the truth in order to draw away disciples after them. So be on your guard! Remember that for three years I never stopped warning each of you night and day with tears. (Acts 19.29-31)

It is just how this world is. From the moment you put your trust in Jesus the Devil will be trying every trick to stop you. Jesus said to his followers just before he was arrested:

Simon, Simon, Satan has asked to sift all of you as wheat. But I have prayed for you, Simon, that your faith may not fail. And when you have turned back, strengthen your brothers. (Luke 22.31,32)

In 1 Peter 5.8,9 we read:

Be alert and of sober mind. Your enemy the devil prowls around like a roaring lion looking for someone to devour. Resist him, standing firm in the faith, because you know that your fellow believers throughout the world are undergoing the same kind of sufferings.

Paul was so exasperated that the people he had brought to faith in Jesus in the region of Galatia had been deceived by false teachers that he wrote:

I am astonished that you are so quickly deserting the one who called you by the grace of Christ and are turning to a different gospel - which is really no gospel at all. Evidently some people are throwing you into confusion and are trying to pervert the gospel of Christ. (Galatians 1.6,7)

And then in his concern for them wrote:

You foolish Galatians! Who has bewitched you? Before your very eyes Jesus Christ was clearly portrayed as crucified. I would like to learn just one thing from you: Did you receive the Spirit by observing the law, or by believing what you heard? Are you so foolish? After beginning with the Spirit, are you now trying to finish by human effort? Have you experienced so much in vain - if it really was in vain? (Galatians 3.1-4)

One of the tricks the Devil uses is seeding attractive but false ideas into people and churches. These weaken people's faith, stop them growing into mature Christians and stop them being effective in God's work. You may well be joining a church that is already infected by one or more of these spiritual viruses. If you have the "antibodies" to protect you from succumbing yourself, that is one person rescued and as you become stronger in Christ you may be able to rescue others.

Despite all these hazards, the person who honestly wants to stick with Christ will ultimately be kept safe. As Jesus said:

My sheep listen to my voice; I know them, and they follow me. I give them eternal life, and they shall never perish; no one will snatch them out of my hand. My Father, who has given them to me, is greater than all; no one can snatch them out of my Father's hand. I and the Father are one. (John 10.27-29)

So do not be afraid, but do be on your guard. Let us start by looking at the three things I think I can safely say every Christian needs: interaction with other believers, the Bible and a prayer life. Here is a good place to say a little bit about each of these. Actually, I want to say more than just 'a little bit' so I will give each one a chapter to itself.

PART TWO

THREE THINGS EVERY CHRISTIAN NEEDS

CHAPTER THREE

Community

Finding A Church

As the poet John Donne said, "no man is an island." We need other people. In normal circumstances you need to be part of a group of believers, whatever shape this group takes; be it a church, a bible study or prayer group, or even just your family. That is just basic sociology!

So, let us say you start to go to a local church of your chosen denomination. From personal experience I suggest you first ask God what church he would like you to join. He is undoubtedly the One who best knows what would suit you, and suit his plans involving you.

God likes us to ask, and when we do he responds. Exactly what means he will use to guide you when you ask, I do not know. However, I can say that looking back on my life, when I asked that question he managed to get me safely there (looking back I also have to say that sometimes if I had not been quite so pig-headed he would have gotten me there much sooner).

When you go to a church what will you find?

a) You will find people. Some, like you, will be baby Christians. Some will have been Christians for a long time, and in that time grown perhaps a lot or perhaps only a little into maturity in Christ. Some sadly may never have seen beyond mere religious observances to choosing God as described in the previous section. All these are your new spiritual family! God will work through them to help look after you, and God will also work through you to help look after them.

b) You will find human traditions. They may be centuries old like the Anglican prayer book or the Roman Catholic tradition of celibate priests. Or they may be only years old like "in our church we always have half an hour of worship (by which they mean singing) then the announcements, then the sermon". Or even perhaps "Our tradition is to reject all tradition". Any sort can be a help or a hindrance. Any sort can be biblical or un-biblical. Any sort can become like the traditions of Jesus' day which made Jesus say that their religious traditions were the opposite of God's commands:

> So the Pharisees and teachers of the law asked Jesus, 'Why don't your disciples live according to the tradition of the elders instead of eating their food with defiled hands?' He replied, 'Isaiah was right when he prophesied about you hypocrites; as it is written:
> 'These people honor me with their lips,
> but their hearts are far from me.
> They worship me in vain;
> their teachings are merely human rules.'
> You have let go of the commands of God and are holding on to human traditions.'
> And he continued, 'You have a fine way of setting aside the commands of God in order to observe your own traditions! For Moses said, 'Honor your father and mother,' and, 'Anyone who curses their father or

mother is to be put to death.' But you say that if anyone declares that what might have been used to help their father or mother is Corban (that is, devoted to God)— then you no longer let them do anything for their father or mother. Thus you nullify the word of God by your tradition that you have handed down. And you do many things like that. (Mark 7.5-13)

Be very careful about religious traditions. Check them out against what the Bible teaches and never let go of the commands of God to hold onto human traditions.

c) You will find clergy. The "good" ones may be outstanding men or women of God or they may just be more ordinary believers who are doing faithful if unspectacular work for God. In either case give them due respect: God is holding them responsible for your spiritual welfare just as in olden times a shepherd was held responsible by the owner for the care of his sheep. So be tolerant of their human foibles, and their incomplete knowledge, even of things spiritual. Just remember how even the best parents don't know everything or get everything right, but they still looked after you and bring you up.

But there are two other classes of clergy that require more caution. Jesus said:

"Many will say to me on that day, 'Lord, Lord, did we not prophesy in your name and in your name drive out demons and in your name perform many miracles?' Then I will tell them plainly, 'I never knew you. Away from me, you evildoers!'" (Matthew 7.22, 23)

There are clergy, even bishops, famous platform speakers and tele-evangelists who will one day be condemned by Jesus. Some, for all that they talk about "God", resemble the before picture of people who have come to Christ, not the after picture! They are people whose lives are dominated by their old human natures, not by the Holy Spirit.

Others are imitating the false prophets of Old Testament days. The Old Testament is full of examples of the religious professionals of that time (prophets and priests) who claimed to be speaking for God but who were actively misleading the people and frequently bitterly opposing the real messengers God had sent.

I will give just two examples for now although you will come across many more as you read the Bible. First where the real messenger of God, Jeremiah, is flogged on the orders of the head priest.

> When the priest Pashhur son of Immer, the official in charge of the temple of the LORD, heard Jeremiah prophesying these things, he had Jeremiah the prophet beaten and put in the stocks at the Upper Gate of Benjamin at the LORD's temple. (Jeremiah 20.1)

Second where Jeremiah delivers a message from God giving God's opinion of the religious leaders:

> "Both prophet and priest are godless;
> even in my temple I find their wickedness,"
> declares the LORD.
> "And among the prophets of Jerusalem
> I have seen something horrible:
> They commit adultery and live a lie.
> They strengthen the hands of evildoers,
> so that not one of them turns from their wickedness."
> This is what the LORD Almighty says:
> "Do not listen to what the prophets are prophesying to you;
> they fill you with false hopes.
> They speak visions from their own minds,

not from the mouth of the LORD.
They keep saying to those who despise me,
'The LORD says: You will have peace.'
And to all who follow the stubbornness of their hearts
they say, 'No harm will come to you.'
But which of them has stood in the council of the
LORD to see or to hear his word?
    I did not send these prophets,
yet they have run with their message;
I did not speak to them,
yet they have prophesied.
But if they had stood in my council,
they would have proclaimed my words to my people
and would have turned them from their evil ways
and from their evil deeds." (Jeremiah 23.11-22)

The recurring theme here is that the religious professionals should have been speaking out to turn the people from their evil ways. Instead they were telling people that they had nothing to fear, God would never punish them. God gave them (and us) a graphic demonstration during Jeremiah's time that he does punish. He sent the Babylonian army against his people. Jerusalem was destroyed and the people carried off into exile. Think about current church ministers and leaders. How many of them are trying to turn people from their evil ways? How many of them are spreading the false message "God will not punish"?

(Caution: I may have oversimplified this! What I mean is: Jesus was really strong on the message of God punishing, yes: - but mainly to the religious people like the Pharisees who mistakenly thought God approved of them! To the sinners and tax gatherers he exemplified God's love and mercy - not denouncing their sins but showing them the way back to God, and they then joyfully gave up the evil of their old ways.)

The last group of clergy are mercifully rare - but be on the lookout. These are the ones who are evil even by the standards of the world, for example the pedophiles and the senior church leaders who tried to hide the pedophiles' crimes.

I really do not believe that some of these church officials know God at all! Those church officials who caused further suffering to the victims by refusing to listen to their allegations and those who tried to cover up the pedophiles' crimes "for the sake of the church" - if they had believed anything of what the Bible says about God's character they would have been far too afraid of him to do that!

Jesus said, "It would be better for them to be thrown into the sea with a millstone tied around their neck than to cause one of these little ones to stumble." (Luke 17.2) And in Psalm 11.5 "The LORD examines the righteous, but the wicked, those who love violence, he hates with a passion." Hebrews 10.30,31 says: "For we know him who said, 'It is mine to avenge; I will repay' ... It is a dreadful thing to fall into the hands of the living God."

So you need to be prepared for what you will meet when you join a church, but problems with individuals should not keep you from Christian fellowship altogether. I am very sorry if you have been burnt by a group calling themselves Christians, but if you can find a new community you will grow and flourish so much faster and stronger in your faith.

CHAPTER FOUR

Bible Reading

The Importance of The Bible

If you want to know what God is like and how he wants us to live the primary and only authoritative source of information is the Bible. As a brand new baby Christian you may need at first to imbibe the Bible's teaching in a regurgitated form from older Christians who are acting like spiritual parents towards you. But all the same you need to grow up and get reading it for yourself as soon as you can.

Because the Bible is so vital to spiritual growth be warned that the Devil will try to stop you reading it. Beware of anyone trying to get you off reading the Bible itself and on to reading books (or watching to DVD's) about the Bible. Christian books and video sermons and the like can be helpful but never, never as a substitute for reading the Bible itself! The Bible really is God's word ... anything else is anyone's guess.

Historically one ploy of the Devil to turn people away from the Bible was to keep the Bible out of the language ordinary people spoke. In the Middle Ages when the Bible was in Latin, only the priests and scholars could read it - and the people had to believe their interpretation of it. Around the 1400's people who tried to translate the Bible into English and distribute it were burned at the stake by church authorities. Eventually in England every church had to have a Bible in English where anyone could come in and read it for themselves, and it had to be read to the people at every service. This was a radical and tremendously important breakthrough and gave rise to a resurgence of belief throughout England.

Nowadays some tele-evangelists and ministers who imitate them are trying to turn the clock back to be in the position of medieval priests. They tell their people only to read the King James Version - which is so different to modern English that most people have serious trouble understanding it, so are forced to rely on these new medieval priests to translate it for them.

As an aside, this applies mostly to the post World War II generations. My 98 year old mother was brought up on the KJV and does understand its language. She probably does not realise that she was at the same time taught sufficient ancient Greek and Hebrew grammar and idiom to make it understandable. For instance she may not know that "-im" is the usual Hebrew plural ending (like "s" in English) but she certainly understands "cherubim and seraphim" to mean the plural.

However the barely literate 13 year old girl who once proudly told me "The King James Bible is good enough for [named famous tele-evangelist] so it is good enough for me!" certainly could not understand it!

Don't let tricksters fool you. Get a copy of the Bible in language you can understand! And don't let anyone tell you this is less authentic. The New Testament was originally written in the worldwide trade version of ancient Greek. The purpose was so that ordinary people everywhere could understand it. Get a Bible you can read and understand!

Two translations I find useful are (a) the *New Living* for reading large slabs because it has tried to use modern English expressions and (b) the *TNIV* (Today's New International Version) which is slower reading because it still carries over a little bit of Hebrew and Greek grammar and idioms which are not used in modern English. But as you progress in your study of the Bible or if you've actually studied Greek and Hebrew at some stage, these versions do add to the vividness and show you where you need to pause and think about double meanings etc. The *New RSV* (New Revised Standard Version) is like *TNIV* only I think it is harder for modern English speakers to understand because it carries over more of the Greek and Hebrew way of expressing ideas rather than translating them into English, and its clunky to read. Having said that if you find it suits you then use it.

Those are my favourites. But what I am really trying to say is that you should find translations that use the sort of language you use every day and that you find easy to read and understand.

Where To Start

My personal suggestion is to make a start with the New Testament and try to read through to the end even if some bits you find perplexing. One reason I say this is that even a good human teacher makes their point many times in different ways. People are different and some will understand a thing most easily when it is explained in one way, and other people will understand it most easily when it is explained in another. If humans are smart enough to know that, then we should expect the same of God who is smarter than the best human speaker and at the same time understands human nature better than anyone else. We should expect God to have all his important themes stated in the Bible multiple times in different ways to get through to different people.

So a thing may seem puzzling because it is a puzzle or it may just be that it seems puzzling because it is being presented in a way that doesn't click with your personality but does for other people. In the latter case reading on is sensible on the basis that somewhere else it will be presented in a way that you will find easy to absorb. Then next time you read through you will be able to see what the formerly puzzling bit means because you have already learned what it is teaching in another part of the Bible.

The Old Testament is important. It is inspired by the same God and teaches the same things about God and humans and how God wants us to live. Don't let anyone lead you astray by trying to carve off the Old Testament from the New - the Bible is both together! As with reading the New Testament, the important thing at first is to get an overview and a feel for the general sort of things it teaches. Because the important lessons are repeated over and over, a quick read through - yes even skipping the boring bits - for the first, and maybe even second and third time will help your understanding, and knowing your O.T. will protect you from con artists.

How To Use The Bible

Here is an example of a false teacher who claimed the spiritual life of one of my recently converted people years ago. Let us call this new convert "Fred". Fred came up to me after church and told me that

I had gotten it all wrong about prayer. He had been reading books that had let him see the truth. He explained this "truth" which basically boiled down to this proposition "We are the masters and God is our slave. We must command God to do what we want."

Boiled down to its basics I hope all of you can see that this is the exact opposite of what the Bible teaches! Of course the books he read will have built up to it much more subtly, and I suppose they wound him in like a fisherman gently reeling in a fish until it can be scooped into the boat. But if Fred had read big chunks of his Bible he would have felt there was something wrong straight away. But he hadn't and he didn't.

When I tried to reason with him, Fred said it was what the Bible said. Fred then quoted his proof text "Thus saith the Lord ... concerning the work of my hands command ye me". There you are: we are told to command God what to do! Point proved. Case closed! Or was it ...

Remember I warned you against people who insist on only the King James Version. Well, those words only appear in the KJV. Keep in mind that the KJV was created before a lot of early Greek texts were rediscovered, and so more recent translations have cut out verses which don't appear to have good support in the earliest Greek manuscripts. Therefore, be wary of verses that only appear in the KJV. Further, charlatans love to use it because it's not in understandable language and unscrupulous people can put their spin on it and their victims can't tell it's just spin.

Warning bell No. 1: Beware the quotation from obsolete or oddball translations.

Solution: check a couple of different modern translations!

Quoting a short string of words out of the Bible is not quoting the Bible. What I mean is the Bible is a big book, it is not that hard if you look far enough for you to find a string of words in it that taken just on their own can say just about anything. Put them back in their context as part of a chapter or a whole narrative and they don't mean that at all. It is a favourite trick of people from complete charlatans to otherwise honest folk who want to get an edge in an argument to delve into the Bible and dig out soundbites. Soundbites work. They stick in people's heads, they win arguments. But that way the Bible can be made out to say just about anything.

Warning bell No.2: Short quotations are often misquotations!

Solution: read a slice either side until you can see what the whole passage of the Bible is saying.

In arguments people often use what are called "proof texts" - short snappy Bible quotes that look like they settle the argument. As soundbites they are very catchy and hence effective: that is why people use them! However, as a means to understanding what the Bible actually teaches they are often very misleading. So for a start check all quotes out in their context.

Caution: Jesus used one-liners BUT very differently! He did it as a memory trigger to the whole section where the Bible was teaching a certain thing. It's a lot like quoting lines for films, which my family love to do. When we do we are trying to bring to mind the situation in the film where that quote occurs, not just conveying the face value of the words of the quote. My feeling is that the Bible writers use short scripture quotes in the same sort of way. So you need to know the context in order to get the quote!

Also, just as "one swallow doesn't make a spring", one statement in the Bible, even if you have checked the two warnings above, cannot establish anything important. No human speaker would make an important point only once, so why would God? As I have already said (see, even I do it!) the important lessons run like a thread right through the Bible.

And again some parts of the Bible are hard to understand. Also some passages of the Bible could support any one of several different interpretations.

The accepted rules for these instances are:

1. Use the really clear bits of the Bible to set the interpretation of difficult or ambiguous bits.

2. Never accept an interpretation of one part of the Bible which means the opposite of what the Bible says in other parts.

Warning Bell No.3: There appears to be only one part of the Bible that supports the idea.

Solution: Remember that important lessons are repeated over and over again in the Bible. If you are reading slabs of the Bible you will automatically (and the Holy Spirit will help you too) start get a feel for what is important.

The Three Warning Bells

So let me play out the three warning bells in this case. I'll go from 3 to 1 for some dramatic effect.

Warning Bell 3: Does that teaching crop up all through the Bible? ...

Fred has read this "wonderful" book that tells him that we humans should give the orders and God should obey them. Proof text "Command ye me saith the Lord" (Isaiah 41.11(b)). Even if you have only read a tiny bit of the Bible does that sound right? No! You can't get very far in the Bible without finding that we humans are meant to obey God not the other way round! (If you need an example, read through John chapters 14 & 15 and see how many times Jesus things like "if you love me you will obey my commandments"!)

So Fred should have been on guard, he should have suspected he was being deceived into deserting God. Then he could have done some digging for himself in the Bible and really quickly satisfied himself that obedience to God's commands is what the Bible teaches, and he could have thrown that book out. But he didn't.

Warning Bell 2: Do the words bear that interpretation in context ...

Fred has been sold on this slice of words "command ye me saith the Lord" with the interpretation that God says that we are his masters and inviting us to give him our orders. Well, those words, cut out as they are from any background, could mean that. They are in KJV English and our language has changed so much in 400 years that we may be totally misunderstanding even these words, but for the moment we will play along with the trickster and use the KJV ourselves. Oh yes, we can beat this one even playing with his loaded dice!

Look at Isaiah 45 in KJV. (I will summarize some bits but feel free to check for yourself)

Chapter 40 in Isaiah heralds a change in theme from events of King Hezekiah's time before the Babylonians destroyed Jerusalem and took the people off into exile, to a message of hope for the survivors some 70 years later and getting them ready for God's plan to bring them back to Jerusalem. Chapter 40 begins with the stirring "Comfort, comfort my people ... Tell them ... Their warfare is ended ... they have been paid double for all their sins ... make a highway in the desert ... Tell the towns of Judah 'Your God is coming'..." and then it talks about how much greater God is than the "gods" of the nations.

By chapter 43 God is assuring them that he has it all planned, he is going to destroy the Babylonians who took them captive. God has ordained it that Jerusalem will be rebuilt.

Then God drops the bombshell at the beginning of chapter 45: he is going to do this by the hand of Cyrus the Persian, a pagan who does not even know God exists! I am going to suggest that that would be a real problem for the devout Jews who heard it. I am going to suggest that the next section - which I will paste in from the KJV - is God saying essentially "look people, it's my way or ... my way! I AM God!"

> Woe unto him that striveth with his Maker! Let the potsherd strive with the potsherds of the earth. Shall the clay say to him that fashioneth it, What makest thou? or thy work, He hath no hands?

> Woe unto him that saith unto his father, What begettest thou? or to the woman, What hast thou brought forth?

> Thus saith the LORD, the Holy One of Israel, and his Maker, Ask me of things to come concerning my sons, and concerning the work of my hands command ye me.

> I have made the earth, and created man upon it: I, even my hands, have stretched out the heavens, and all their host have I commanded.

> I have raised him up in righteousness, and I will direct all his ways: he shall build my city, and he shall let go my captives, not for price nor reward, saith the LORD of hosts. (Isaiah 45.9-13)

So even in KJV that word string "command ye me" at the end of verse 11 cannot mean what the false teachers were claiming! Is God inviting them to tell him how to run the show? Not at all! Right from saying clay doesn't tell the potter what to do (v 9) through to "I have raised him (Cyrus) up and I will direct all his ways: he shall build my city (Jerusalem), and he shall let go my captives (the Jews)" the message is: God makes the rules!

So "concerning the work of my hands command ye me" has to be an almost incredulous question with the answer implied: No! Don't even think about it!

Warning Bell 1: Try other translations ...

I had to save this till last because it would have blown their claim out of the water straight off. That would have been too simple!

Look at just v. 11 from some other translations:

New Living Bible
This is what the Lord says—
the Holy One of Israel and your Creator:
"Do you question what I do for my children?
Do you give me orders about the work of my hands?"

Contemporary English Version
I am the LORD, the Creator, the holy God of Israel.
Do you dare question me about my own nation
or about what I have done?

TNIV
This is what the LORD says—
the Holy One of Israel, and its Maker:
Concerning things to come,
do you question me about my children,
or give me orders about the work of my hands?

How did it end for Fred? I tried to explain the true situation from the Bible but he had already been hooked. That is one reason I am writing this book, in my experience once people have been hooked by false teaching they frequently cannot hear the truth. As I stood there, open Bible in my hand pointing out what it really said, he replied simply: "this bible teacher has a multi-million dollar TV ministry: you just have a small church. I must believe him!" Some months later Fred (by then openly contemptuous of our "spiritual inferiority") left our church, and I never saw him again.

The best way to safe guard against this type of deception is therefore to consult your Bible before believing it. It is your responsibility to test out the truth of what is told to you, even by teachers that seem to be generally trustworthy.

CHAPTER FIVE

Prayer Life

The Need To Communicate

Part of being a Christian is developing our relationship with God. Part of developing any relationship is communicating. Us communicating to God is called praying. It doesn't have to be in fancy language: you wouldn't try that on your human friends! It doesn't always have to be in words even. The important thing is communicating.

Where is God while you are talking to him? You are now a child of God; the Holy Spirit now lives in you (being spirit he can do that and live simultaneously in any number of other people). So your prayers don't have to go anywhere, God has come to you.

True, you cannot tell God anything he doesn't already know, but he still likes you to tell him. That is how relationships grow. Also part of telling him things is for our benefit. He is day by day changing our attitudes and habits of mind to make us the person he would like us to be. That is to be a person who is uniquely "us" but who is imitating Jesus in all important aspects. As we tell him how we see things, if we will let him he can start to help us understand how he sees them, and that is really important in our growth.

Yes, of course God knows what we need before we ask. That is not the point. The point is we are developing a relationship with him. He likes us to ask! One reason is given in Psalm 50.15 "and call on me in the day of trouble; I will deliver you, and you will honour me." When we ask and he helps us, we know it was him and can honour him for it.

Another reason is that asking can be a growth experience. Will God give you anything you ask for? No. I don't mean God ever lacks the power to do anything he wishes to do. That is never his situation. But there are reasons why he will not do everything we ask. Here are some common ones:-

1. God is utterly good, and there are many things we humans do, and may ask him to do, which he would never even think of doing. God would never tell a lie. God would never break a promise. God would never do anything unfair or unjust. As baby Christians some of our prayers are going to be for things that seemed OK to us before we became Christians, but which are not God's way of doing things. If we pray for these things, God will not do them - no matter how grand a tantrum we throw - and that can be a learning opportunity for us.

2. We are spiritual babies. Even human parents safeguard their children by saying "No" to requests that would be dangerous. Suppose a child saw their parent preparing dinner with a sharp knife and wanted mummy or daddy to give them the knife to play with. Would a good parent give it to them?

3. We never know everything. We will to the end of our days be asking God to do things we think would be good which he does not do. Sometimes we get to look back and realise "Am I ever glad God did not answer that prayer! What I wanted then would have

been a disaster." Sometimes we don't get this hindsight and just have to trust that he knew something we didn't.

The best human parents will often refuse to give their child junk food just before dinner, or let them watch just one more TV show before bed no matter how much their child demands it. But should that same parent hear a scream of terror from their child they will come running, prepared to fight to the death to save their baby. God is to us a perfect parent. There are things he will not do no matter how much or how well we pray. But even the most inarticulate desperate cry to him for help from one of his little ones can result in a more powerful miracle than the prayers of some great saint would.

Similarly, there is nothing we can ask God to do for others or for his work in the world that he could not perform without our asking. But he seems to like to take us into a sort of junior partnership, where parts of his work he shares with us by letting us ask, and then he does the part requiring his power. One example from the Bible is Paul's request for the believers to pray for his work spreading the gospel:

> Devote yourselves to prayer, being watchful and thankful. And pray for us, too, that God may open a door for our message, so that we may proclaim the mystery of Christ, for which I am in chains. Pray that I may proclaim it clearly, as I should. (Colossians 4.2-4)

When you pray for something, you are entering into a partnership with God, which is a great way to strength and develop your relationship. Just remember that the best outcome is understanding and being closer to God, not always getting what you want. So don't be discouraged if you think God hasn't answered your prayers. He has, the answer was just either "no" or "not yet". From either of these answers you can learn a lot, if you take the time. So don't give up on praying.

Abuses of Prayer

There are at least three common abuses of prayer you are likely to encounter, which I want to highlight so you can protect against them.

Prayer To Manipulate

A) Treating prayer as a way to manipulate God to get what we want, not as part of our relationship with a loving heavenly father.

At the light end of this practice, people can talk about "prayer achieving this or that". It then develops into an attitude that somehow we make it happen by doing this thing called prayer. It is a bad attitude, and really needs to be nipped in the bud. It is God who does things. When he lets us share his work by letting us pray, or prompting us to pray and then doing his act of power, it is thrilling and exciting and wonderful - just as long as we remember to picture ourselves as the toddler "helping" daddy carry the heavy bucket of water! It is a thing God is doing with us because that is the sort of thing that good fathers and their little kids do together.

Just remember NOT to imitate the spoilt toddler who throws a tantrum because daddy steers the bucket to the rose garden not to the mud pit the toddler wants to make to play in! Spiritually, just as humanly, that behaviour is bound to end in tears!

At the really bad end we end up trying to be magicians - using prayer as some sort of magic to bring about what we want supernaturally regardless of God's purposes. This one does not just end in tears: unless we are rescued, it ends in hell!

There is a great description of an event in Acts that resulted in converts confessing that they had just added Christianity to their store of magic. Though luckily, in this instance they repented.

> Some Jews who went around driving out evil spirits tried to invoke the name of the Lord Jesus over those who were demon-possessed. They would say, "In the name of the Jesus whom Paul preaches, I command you to come out." Seven sons of Sceva, a Jewish chief priest, were doing this. One day the evil spirit answered them, "Jesus I know, and Paul I know about, but who are you?" Then the man who had the evil spirit jumped on them and overpowered them all. He gave them such a beating that they ran out of the house naked and bleeding.
>
> When this became known to the Jews and Greeks living in Ephesus, they were all seized with fear, and the name of the Lord Jesus was held in high honor. Many of those who believed now came and openly confessed what they had done. A number who had practiced sorcery brought their scrolls together and burned them publicly. When they calculated the value of the scrolls, the total came to fifty thousand drachmas. In this way the word of the Lord spread widely and grew in power. (Acts 19. 13-20)

An example of the difference between what the Bible means by prayer and what people often mistake it as can be found in 1 Kings 18. The King of Israel had married a feisty foreign princess named Jezebel. She worshiped the Sidonian god Baal, who they thought controlled the weather. Jezebel promoted Baal worship in Israel, and after she had either killed or forced into hiding all the ministers of God, Baal worship took over. God sent his prophet Elijah to throw down the gauntlet by announcing a drought.

After three years with no rain Elijah challenged the king to assemble all the ministers of Baal to a contest on Mount Carmel. They could build an altar to Baal but not light the fire. He would build an altar to God, but not light the fire. The ministers of Baal would pray, Elijah would pray. The deity that answered by setting fire to his altar was the real god. This is a slightly long quote, but so much fun that I've left it all in.

Then Elijah said to the prophets of Baal, "You go first, for there are many of you. Choose one of the bulls, and prepare it and call on the name of your god. But do not set fire to the wood."

So they prepared one of the bulls and placed it on the altar. Then they called on the name of Baal from morning until noontime, shouting, "O Baal, answer us!" But there was no reply of any kind. Then they danced, hobbling around the altar they had made.

About noontime Elijah began mocking them. "You'll have to shout louder," he scoffed, "for surely he is a god! Perhaps he is daydreaming, or is relieving himself. Or maybe he is away on a trip, or is asleep and needs to be wakened!"

So they shouted louder, and following their normal custom, they cut themselves with knives and swords until the blood gushed out. They raved all afternoon until the time of the evening sacrifice, but still there was no sound, no reply, no response.

Then Elijah called to the people, "Come over here!" They all crowded around him as he repaired the altar of the Lord that had been torn down. He took twelve stones, one to represent each of the tribes of Israel, and he used the stones to rebuild the altar in the name of the Lord. Then he dug a trench around the altar large enough to hold about three gallons. He piled wood on the altar, cut the bull into pieces, and laid the pieces on the wood.

Then he said, "Fill four large jars with water, and pour the water over the offering and the wood."

After they had done this, he said, "Do the same thing again!" And when they were finished, he said, "Now do it a third time!" So they did as he said, and the water ran around the altar and even filled the trench.

At the usual time for offering the evening sacrifice, Elijah the prophet walked up to the altar and prayed, "O Lord, God of Abraham, Isaac, and Jacob, prove today that you are God in Israel and that I am your servant. Prove that I have done all this at your command. O Lord, answer me! Answer me so these people will know that you, O Lord, are God and that you have brought them back to yourself."

Immediately the fire of the Lord flashed down from heaven and burned up the young bull, the wood, the stones, and the dust. It even licked up all the water in the trench! And when all the people saw it, they fell face down on the ground and cried out, "The Lord—he is God! Yes, the Lord is God!" (1 Kings 18. 25-39)

The ministers of Baal thought "prayer" worked (in the magic sense) and they did it with a passion, and all day - but nothing happened. Elijah believed God had sent him with instructions to set up this contest so that God could perform a great sign to convince the people and that God could be trusted to carry out his part. His prayer was simple, short and said plainly. The answer was a really spectacular miracle.

Content-less Prayer

B) Praying excessively without actually saying anything.

You will hear this in the public prayers in many churches. Now of course public prayer is a bit different to private prayer. It is corporate, it is the action of a body of believers, even though just one person may be saying the words. So the person saying the prayer does have to be careful to pray things the whole body of believers can say "Amen" to. That does limit what one aught to pray for publicly. However, you still have to be specific about what you are asking God to do. Prayers that run like "We pray for the church in Africa, we pray for the United Nations, we pray for ..." are like posting letters without writing anything on the inside.

So if you are to pray for, say, the church in Africa, well what do you as a congregation want God to do for your brothers and sisters there? I suspect the lack of content of these prayers is often the result of a lack of belief that God is real or capable of doing anything.

For an example of public prayer that does have content the old Anglican prayer book is a good model. The authors managed to compose prayers that were so general they could be used in different situations, century after century but which still asked God to do something. If we are going to pray in church for current circumstances and the present needs of others we should be able to do better, not worse than this model!

Here is just one example:

Almighty and everliving God,
who by thy holy Apostle hast taught us to make prayers, and supplications, and to give thanks for all men;

We humbly beseech thee most mercifully to receive these our prayers, which we offer unto thy Divine Majesty;

beseeching thee to inspire continually the Universal Church with the spirit of truth, unity, and concord:

And grant, that all they who do confess thy holy Name may agree in the truth of thy holy Word, and live in unity, and godly love.

We beseech thee also to save and defend all Christian Kings, Princes, and Governors; and specially thy Servant ELIZABETH our Queen; that under her we may be godly and quietly governed:

And grant unto her whole Council, and to all that are put in authority under her, that they may truly and impartially administer justice, to the punishment of wickedness and vice, and to the maintenance of thy true religion, and virtue.

Give grace, O heavenly Father, to all Bishops and Curates, that they may both by their life and doctrine set forth thy true and lively Word, and rightly and duly administer thy holy Sacraments.

And to all thy people give thy heavenly grace; and especially to this congregation here present; that, with meek heart and due reverence, they may hear, and receive thy holy Word; truly serving thee in holiness and righteousness all the days of their life.

And we most humbly beseech thee, of thy goodness, O Lord, to comfort and succour all those who, in this transitory life, are in trouble, sorrow, need, sickness, or any other adversity.

And we also bless thy holy Name for all thy servants departed this life in thy faith and fear; beseeching thee to give us grace so to follow their good examples, that with them we may be partakers of thy heavenly kingdom.

Grant this, O Father, for Jesus Christ's sake, our only Mediator and Advocate. Amen.

So, if you really believed God will act, how would this change the content of your prayers?

Prayer To Others

C) Praying to something other than God.

Over the years we have had various Roman Catholic friends who were a great inspiration and model to us for the way they could talk freely and naturally about their Christian faith. But all the same, some of them have had attitudes to prayer that were not good. I know they were just doing what they were taught from the cradle, and indeed God seemed to cut them a great deal of slack and obviously answered their prayers! But that is no excuse for anyone else to adopt habits of prayer that the Bible clearly shows are deficient if not downright forbidden!

One dear lady used to pray to her dead mother-in-law instead of directly to God. The reasoning went like this: Mother-in-law was a good woman so she would be in heaven and be able to take it up with Mary, and then if Mary asked Jesus, well since he was a good son he would do what his mother asked! OK that is very human but it is also very wrong!

What does the Bible say?

1) We are adopted sons and daughters with direct access to God the Father, Son and Holy Spirit. So we should honour God for bringing us into this wonderful sphere of grace by making use of it and praying direct to God.

> Yet to all who did receive him, to those who believed in his name, he gave the right to become children of God - children born not of natural descent,

nor of human decision or a husband's will, but born of God. (John 1.12,13)

For those who are led by the Spirit of God are the children of God. The Spirit you received does not make you slaves, so that you live in fear again; rather, the Spirit you received brought about your adoption to sonship. And by him we cry, "Abba, Father." The Spirit himself testifies with our spirit that we are God's children. (Romans 8.14-16)

For through him (Jesus) we both have access to the Father by one Spirit. (Ephesians 2.18)

2.) Jesus told us that the Holy Spirit would come and dwell in our hearts, and through the Spirit he and the Father would be in us. So we can pray to Father, Son and Holy Spirit because they are in us. We cannot pray to dead people, even saints or Mary because they do not live in us!

If you love me, keep my commands. And I will ask the Father, and he will give you another advocate to help you and be with you forever— the Spirit of truth. The world cannot accept him, because it neither sees him nor knows him. But you know him, for he lives with you and will be in you. I will not leave you as orphans; I will come to you." ... 23 Jesus replied, "Anyone who loves me will obey my teaching. My Father will love them, and we will come to them and make our home with them. (John 15.16-23)

3.) We are strictly forbidden in the Bible from trying to talk to dead people. This is especially true when we are trying to talk to God.

When someone tells you to consult mediums and spiritists, who whisper and mutter, should not a people inquire of their God? Why consult the dead on behalf of the living? (Isaiah 8.19)

4.) It can lead to giving glory to something other than God, which God hates. One example of this kind of prayer was told to us in all seriousness while my wife and I were travelling. When we visited the island of Corfu we were told of the deliverance of the city during the Ottoman attack in 1716. Here is a clip from the Wikipedia article:

> "After a great storm on 9 August - which the defenders attributed to the intervention of Corfu's patron saint, Saint Spyridon - caused great casualties among the besiegers, the siege was broken off on 11 August and the last Ottoman forces withdrew on 20 August"

The defenders had apparently been praying for deliverance, but when there was great storm which caused the attackers to retreat did they attribute it to God? No! What they did (and still do) was to praise St Spyridon, who had been dead for around 1,500 years, for it! His coffin is in the church in the city to this day with a continuous line of people filing past presumably praying to his corpse.

This is not Christianity! It is human religion pretending to be Christian. Spyridon (AD 270 – 348) himself was by all accounts a fine Christian, in which case we can say he is now with Christ in heaven. The corpse in the casket is not the living Spyridon, it is just human remains. However, it has become an idol for the people in the town because they come to it not God. And if there is anything spiritual associated with it then according to the Bible it is a demon:

They made him jealous with their foreign gods and angered him with their detestable idols. They sacrificed to demons, which are not God - (Deuteronomy 32.16,17)

The sacrifices of pagans are offered to demons, not to God, and I do not want you to be participants with demons. (1 Corinthians 10.20)

What does the Bible say about how God views this sort of behaviour?

Do not follow other gods, the gods of the peoples around you; for the LORD your God, who is among you, is a jealous God and his anger will burn against you, and he will destroy you from the face of the land. (Deuteronomy 6.14)

I am the LORD; that is my name!
I will not yield my glory to another
or my praise to idols. (Isaiah 42:8)

So, if you are going to pray: pray to God, Father, Son, Holy Spirit. If you are going to give praise for answered prayer: give it to God alone. Anything else is idolatry!

On A Positive Note

I should not, of course, leave the topic of our prayer life without pasting in some of Jesus's teaching from Matthew 6.5-14. Who better to tell us about how to pray?

When you pray, don't be like the hypocrites who love to pray publicly on street corners and in the synagogues where everyone can see them. I tell you the truth, that is all the reward they will ever get. But when you pray, go away by yourself, shut the door behind you, and pray to your Father in private. Then your Father, who sees everything, will reward you.

When you pray, don't babble on and on as people of other religions do. They think their prayers are answered merely by repeating their words again and again. Don't be like them, for your Father knows exactly what you need even before you ask him! Pray like this:

Our Father in heaven,
may your name be kept holy.
May your Kingdom come soon.
May your will be done on earth,
as it is in heaven.
Give us today the food we need,
and forgive us our sins,
as we have forgiven those who sin against us.
And don't let us yield to temptation,
but rescue us from the evil one.

If you forgive those who sin against you, your heavenly Father will forgive you. But if you refuse to forgive others, your Father will not forgive your sins.

The next section deals with some of the more common forms of false teaching today. I will deal with them in three groups. There are many different heresies out there, but often they fall into one of these three groups. So it will help you to recognise other ones if you can understand the underlying wrong idea about God and what God in Christ Jesus has done for us.

PART THREE

HERESIES

CHAPTER SIX

Heresies of the First Kind

Adding To The Gospel

The first kind of heresy comes from adding to the Gospel. Yes, the Gospel does seem too good to be true. How can the real God be so kind, so loving, so gracious, so forgiving, so ... well, so incredibly wonderfully magnificent?

Therefore, fallen human nature has devised many false gods - distorted and deficient pictures of the true God made known to us in Jesus living, dying and rising. To go along with these our fallen human nature has invented new "gospels" which say that to be saved you need faith in Christ Jesus PLUS this, that or the other thing.

In New Testament times the common one was "... plus you must become a full Jew: be circumcised (for men) and obey the Law of Moses". As you read through the New Testament letters you will see how Paul fought tooth and nail against this because he could see (by the Holy Spirit) how destructive it was to the true Gospel.

In medieval times this deficient picture of God was used to make money. Ministers in the church itself went round teaching that faith in Jesus was not enough, that God had not done everything necessary to reconcile humans to himself. They told the people that they needed to buy indulgences from church authorities otherwise they would burn in hell or purgatory. Can you imagine! The effrontery of trying to sell for mere money the free gift of God that Christ bought at the cost of his own life! But that is what they did.

The main forms of this type of wrong thinking about God that I fear you may come in contact with in the modern age are as well as faith in Jesus you need:

1) the evidence of speaking in tongues

2) to join "our" church

3) to be baptised our way (eg. baptised by immersion as an adult).

Or to be a proper Christian (ie. saved) you must:

4) insert fad of the month, for example: give up smoking, be a vegan, supporting a particular political action moment, be thin, etc.

5) believe science is bad and the world was created in 6 days

None of these things is bad in itself, some are neutral and some are in fact good things. BUT once they are added as necessary to salvation, they then become poison. More on that later. So lets look at these common forms of this heresy.

Speaking In Tongues

"You are not a Spirit filled Christian unless you speak in tongues." - Wrong!

Speaking in tongues is one of the gifts of the Holy Spirit, described and attested to in the New Testament. Some TV evangelists, even some whole churches, argue that it is the only evidence we have that a person has received the Holy Spirit, and so every Christian must speak in tongues. They are quite wrong. Further, many of them are so insistent about it that they fall into the heresy of adding to the Gospel. I think the best immunity comes from a better understanding of what the Holy Spirit does in a believer's life. This is not to deny tongues, but to understand its place in describing the work of the Holy Spirit.

First, let's look at how we receive the Holy Spirit and why. John's Gospel is a good place to start. Read John 7.37-39. Jesus says that streams of living water will flow from the person who believes in him. John adds that Jesus meant the Holy Spirit "whom those who believed in him were later to receive". So the grounds for receiving the Holy Spirit is believing in Jesus.

Take a moment to read John Ch.14 and 16.5-15. To summarise some important things Jesus says:

a) The Holy Spirit will be given to those who love Jesus – this love being shown by obedience.

b) The Holy Spirit will teach believers and remind them of Jesus' words.

c) The Holy Spirit will convict the world of guilt in regard to sin, righteousness and judgement.

d) The Spirit will guide believers into all truth by taking what belongs to Jesus and making it known to them.

Luke in his Gospel and the book of Acts tells us more. Luke 24.48,49 tells us that Jesus told the disciples they would be his witnesses, and the Gospel would be preached to all nations but they were to wait; "I am going to send you what my Father has promised; but stay in the city until you have been clothed with power from on high." So, the coming of the Holy Spirit was a) a matter of promise and b) brought the power which was essential to proclaiming the Gospel.

This instruction is repeated in Acts 1:1-5. With the addition that Jesus uses the term "baptism" when he says: "in a few days you will be baptised with the Holy Spirit." Reading on through Acts Ch.2 the coming of the Holy Spirit on the day of Pentecost (a Jewish festival) is described.

For our present discussion I want to highlight three things that we are told here:

i) The believers all "speak in other tongues" but these are foreign languages, and to their amazement visitors in Jerusalem from many different and distant countries hear the believers telling them the great things God has done in their own native languages. These days, when people are on about "speaking in tongues" they usually do not mean a known foreign language, but rather speaking or praying in words that are unintelligible without spiritual interpretation. Therefore, the use of one cannot be directly used to support the use of the other.

ii) One dramatic effect was that Peter got up and boldly and effectively proclaimed that Jesus was God's Messiah - and 2,000 people believed and were baptised that day!

iii) Part of the message was: "Repent and be baptised every one of you in the name of Jesus Christ so that your sins may be forgiven. And you will receive the gift of the Holy Spirit for the promise is to you and your children and to all that are far off."

What I want to highlight is that the really dramatic work of the Holy Spirit here was to cause people to turn to Jesus in repentance and faith for the forgiveness of their sins. Also that the gift of the Holy Spirit is spoken of as the usual and expected follow on. So while you might speak in tongues, the amazing work of the Holy Spirit that should be praised is the turning to Jesus and repenting! If you have already done that, why are you not impressed with that work of the Holy Spirit?

There is truth in the argument that in the early church, speaking in tongues was expected as a sign of receiving the Holy Spirit. In Acts 8 where this does not happen when the Samaritans believe, it is taken to mean that something is wrong. Peter and John go there to pray for them and lay hands on them with the result that the Samaritans then do receive the Holy Spirit. In a similar vein when Peter tells Cornelius and his gathering, who are all non-Jews, about Jesus and the Holy Spirit comes on them while Peter is still speaking that is taken as a convincing sign from God and the Jewish Christians give praise that God has granted life-giving repentance to the gentiles also.

From these texts it is clear that God did utilise speaking in tongues as an instant indication of his Holy Spirit coming into a believer's life. It is also clear that in these cases an instant sign was necessary. So at this stage we should be thinking: "Yes, where necessary to instantly demonstrate his gift of the Holy Spirit, God did use the phenomenon of 'tongues' - so he may well do so whenever that need exists." But this does not mean that he always does so.

Come now to Romans 8. It is a beautiful chapter. Notice as you read through that God Father, Son and Holy Spirit all work to save us. Even though we are looking especially to find out about what the Holy Spirit does, we must not lose sight of the balanced picture Scripture is presenting.

Having done that, notice what is said about how the Holy Spirit helps us. We turned away from our old life as enemies of God, put our trust in Jesus and pledged to obey his teaching. But that is easier said than done! Our old fallen human nature is ever pulling us in the opposite direction. If we cannot prevail against this nature, we will slip back to our old way of life. The Holy Spirit, so long as we actively choose to live by the Spirit, works in us to help us cut loose from these chains of the past and of our fallen nature. This is important, big, totally huge!!!

A line I heard once goes: *The Law bade me crawl but gave me neither arms nor legs: the Gospel bids me fly and gives me wings.*

The Holy Spirit working in and with us to overcome our old nature and change us from the inside out to be ever more like Jesus - that is the being asked to fly and having wings to do it with. This role of the Holy Spirit to help us become Christ-like should not be minimised.

If you are still doubting the importance of this read Galatians 5 from verse 13. It lists the actions that come naturally to us through our fallen nature: sexual immorality, impurity & debauchery, idolatry & witchcraft, hatred, discord, jealousy, fits of rage, selfish ambition, dissensions, factions, envy, drunkenness, orgies and the like.

Then it lists what the Holy Spirit wants to and will produce in us: Love. Joy. Peace. Patience. Kindness. Goodness. Faithfulness. Gentleness. Self-control.

These are called the fruit of the Spirit. The New Testament tells us that we will know who is of God by their fruit. You want evidence that someone has the Holy Spirit? The real evidence of being a Spirit-filled Christian is the extent to which our lives resemble the second list rather than the first one!

One last text, just so I don't set off any warning bells with not enough Scripture. Read Paul's first letter to the Corinthians chapters 12 - 14. Here he is dealing with the Corinthian Christians' problem of thinking that it is all about speaking in tongues (see, this problem has been around for a long time).

His first argument is that indeed the Holy Spirit works in miraculous ways through believers for the benefit of all God's people. But there is a whole list of different ways the Spirit does this and the Spirit chooses whom he works what gift through.

His second argument is that the body of believers is indeed like a body, in that a whole lot of different part are needed for a body to function. If it was just one body-part (ie one spiritual gift) it would not be a functioning body at all. This finishes with him pointing out that the Holy Spirit works in different ways through different people to build up the body of believers. He finishes with the famous question: "does everyone speak in tongues?" Of course not! In the original Greek this verse uses is a grammatical construction know as "a question demanding the answer 'No!'". This can be guessed even without knowledge of Greek from the context. Verses 29 and 30 state "Are all apostles? Are all prophets? Are all teachers? Do all work miracles? Do all have gifts of healing? Do all speak in tongues?". If you are to answer yes to the last one, then you have to answer yes to all of them!

The third argument is found in chapter 13, that Love is the most excellent way of all:

> Love is patient. Love is kind. Love does not envy, it does not boast, it is not self-seeking, it is not easily angered, it keeps no record of wrongs. Love does not delight in evil but rejoices with the truth. It always protects, always trusts, always hopes, always perseveres. Love never fails. (1 Corinthians 13.4-7)

His fourth argument is in chapter 14. Yes, he writes, tongues are a real gift - but a very inferior one to prophecy, so don't forbid it, but don't carry on over it like little kids with a new toy. Grow up!

My conclusion is this: If anyone has repented of their old life, put their faith in Jesus and set their heart to obey him, then on the promise of God - who cannot lie - their sins are forgiven, they are adopted as children of God and they have received the gift of the Holy Spirit. This will be demonstrated first and foremost in the development of the fruits of the Spirit, not one specific gift of the Spirit. From then on they must moment by moment choose to live by the Spirit rather than live according to their old fallen nature. The change may be gradual, but it is the real evidence of the Holy Spirit in their lives.

The One True Church

"You believe in Jesus, great ... But now you need to belong to the True Church" - Wrong!

By the "true church" they mean of course their own denomination or church party. This has been taught by the Roman Catholic church with the catch-cry "Outside the Church (of Rome) there is no salvation". It was taught by the denomination I grew up in (they may have become more broad minded since then). It is said (possibly watered down a teensy bit) by some Pentecostal churches. It is also, I have noticed, implied by some Anglican "flagship" parishes about their own congregation.

It is not true! You are saved by Christ. He saves all those who come to him, not necessarily those who come to any earthly church! If you belong to Christ, then you are a member of his Church - a body of believers stretching through all time and covering all places.

The Bible uses very extravagant language for this Church. In 1 Corinthians it is referred to as the "body of Christ". "Now you are the body of Christ, and each one of you is a part of it." (1 Corinthians 12.27)

1 Peter 2.9,10 says this about us believers in Jesus:

> But you are a chosen people, a royal priesthood, a holy nation, God's special possession, that you may declare the praises of him who called you out of darkness into his wonderful light. Once you were not a people, but now you are the people of God; once you had not received mercy, but now you have received mercy.

Colossians 1.17,18 says Jesus is the head of the Church:

> He is before all things, and in him all things hold together. And he is the head of the body, the church; he is the beginning and the first-born from among the dead, so that in everything he might have the supremacy.

Ephesians 5.25-32 says:

> Husbands, love your wives, just as Christ loved the church and gave himself up for her to make her holy, cleansing her by the washing with water through the word, and to present her to himself as a radiant church, without stain or wrinkle or any other blemish, but holy and blameless. In this same way, husbands ought to love their wives as their own bodies. He who loves his wife loves himself. After all, people have never hated their own bodies, but they feed and care for them, just as Christ does the church— for we are members of his body. For this reason a man will leave his father and mother and be united to his wife, and the two will become one flesh. This is a profound mystery—but I am talking about Christ and the church.

Seriously, do you think any religious institution on earth can fit this description? Rather should we not take Jesus words "My kingdom is not of this world. If it were, my servants would fight to prevent my arrest by the Jewish leaders. But now my kingdom is from another place" (John 18.36) as the true description? His glorious Church is not of this world. Some of his people are still in this world, some are not.

The religious institutions: Roman Catholic, Anglican, Uniting, Greek Orthodox, Assemblies of God, and any other Christian denominations, may under God be of vital assistance to God's people and the spreading of the Gospel and many other worthwhile functions. But not one of them and not even all of them together constitute the "one holy catholic and apostolic Church" of the creed. They are all institutions of this world only, and sadly all too often they run by the power and ideals of our fallen human nature rather than God's Holy Spirit.

So while it is almost certainly God's purpose for you to belong to a congregation of believers and be part of a denomination, remember: you were made a member of God's Church as soon as you came to believe in his son Jesus. Belonging to a particular earthly congregation and denomination is as nothing compared to that.

Baptism

"You believe in Jesus, now you need to be baptised again/by immersion/"believer's baptism"/in our church." - Wrong!

If you have never been baptised at all, then since it is what Christians do, you don't have a problem - go ahead and be baptised. The problem is when you have been baptised as a baby or not baptised by immersion and you come to hear preachers who make it an article of faith that you do it again. The essence of this problem is that baptism in such and such a way becomes a test of whether you are a real Christian. That is, it comes to be added as an article of faith to believing in Christ.

This is the standard line of some more strident evangelical churches. It is very upsetting for Christians in other churches because it is a rather nasty slap in the face: essentially saying "your baptism is not real Christian baptism". Now among more mainline churches, baptism by another church is accepted as "real". If someone I had baptised according to the rites of the Anglican church later joined the Roman Catholic church, they would not re-baptise them, and vice versa. These follow the rule: if you have been baptised with water in the Name of the Father, Son and Holy Spirit, then you have been baptised.

The churches who insist on doing it again generally say it was not real baptism either because it was not done "as a believer" or because it was not by immersion.

Let's look at immersion. The Anglican church is quite in favour of immersion, but does not see it as essential, so for convenience we generally do baptise by pouring water over the candidate's head. This is probably how John the Baptist did it - at least he is depicted baptising that way in some very early Christian art. The Bible does not give any clue as to how he or Jesus did it. The descriptions in the Bible would fit either method! But the real point is that it cannot matter because the Bible does not give instructions to baptise in any particular way, and the Bible was minutely explicit about how to perform ceremonies when it did matter (look at some of the detail given for Old Testament rituals).

I have heard speakers argue that the roots of the Greek word *baptidzo* means to plunge or immerse. Quite right that is one meaning, except that when it had that connotation it meant immerse but not bring up again! When ancient Greek writings said sailors were *baptidzo*-ed they meant they were drowned! That is probably not a meaning we should press.

On the other hand, other uses suggest it can be just a sprinkling. In Mark 7.4 it says: "When they come from the marketplace they do not eat unless they wash. And they observe many other traditions, such as the washing of cups, pitchers and kettles." The Greek word used here for washing is *baptidzo*. You might think it involved full submersion in deep kitchen sinks. However, it appears the custom referred to ceremonially pour water over the outside of the cup only. So we really cannot say from the word *baptidzo* itself how much water "baptising" involved.

The conclusion is that, apart from using water, the Bible is deliberately silent on the mechanics of baptising. So it cannot matter to God. So we should not make the amount of water a matter of dispute.

The other problem is baptising babies. Firstly, "believer's baptism" loses its meaning after a generation or two. I was brought up in a denomination which did not baptise babies, and I served as a priest in a denomination which did. I can say from my observation that it makes no practical difference to the later spiritual life of the individual.

First, even in infant baptism, the adult makes a decision through the confirmation process. Confirmation is where you publicly affirm the baptism promises made on your behalf when you were a baby, and the bishop lays hands on you and prays for you to receive the Holy Spirit. In my early time as an Anglican priest I took confirmation classes. In those days children were sent to confirmation classes at about 15 years of age. In my old denomination children were sent by their parents at about 15 years of age to baptism classes, then for baptism by immersion. Having seen both systems the thing that struck me most forcefully was their complete and utter sameness. Call it "confirmation" or call it "baptism", after a few generations the social function: the degree of belief/unbelief in the kids and the "this is what you do at age 15" -ness was the same in both churches.

Second, infant baptism is still "believer's" baptism - it is in addition taking seriously God's promises in the Bible. One time in my first parish I was having some trouble with parishioners being swayed by "faith healers". I had been watching a video of one and later that week read through the 1662 Prayer Book infant baptism service. (I was not brought up Anglican and by the time I was training there was a new prayer book with a much watered down service so I was not familiar with the original service). The 1662 service sounded to me so much like the faith healers I had been listening to - only the Prayer Book was claiming on behalf of the child things the Bible really does promise.

In the 1662 version of the service Mark 10.13 is read (where Jesus blesses the little children and says "the kingdom of God belongs to such as these") and then the priest reads out:

> BELOVED, ye hear in this Gospel the words of our Saviour Christ, that he commanded the children to be brought unto him; how he blamed those that would have kept them from him; how he exhorted all men to follow their innocency. Ye perceive how by his outward gesture and deed he declared his good will toward

them; for he embraced them in his arms, he laid his hands upon them, and blessed them. Doubt ye not therefore, but earnestly believe, that he hath likewise favourably received this present Infant; that he hath embraced him with the arms of his mercy: and (as he hath promised in his holy Word) will give unto him the blessing of eternal life, and make him partaker of his everlasting kingdom. Wherefore, we being thus persuaded of the good will of our heavenly Father, declared by his Son Jesus Christ, towards this Infant, let us faithfully and devoutly give thanks unto him, and say the Prayer which the Lord himself taught us:

The "doubt ye not but earnestly believe" really struck me. This was faith baptism - believing that Jesus would act now as he did in the Bible narrative, and that he spoke the truth when he said "for the kingdom of God belongs to such as these".

Churches that practice infant baptism do have a rite confirmation where the person is called on to make an adult profession of faith and commitment to Christ. This two part confession of faith: baptism by water and then receiving the Holy Spirit through the laying on of hands, is biblically supported. So, in both the adult baptism and the infant baptism with confirmation there is an adult decision to follow Christ, and both are supported in Scripture.

I am now going to say a strange thing. The only winning move in de-fusing this question as a human addition to the Gospel, and so a heresy, is simply this: do not to buy into the dispute.

Paul spoke to a similar concern of his day when some people thought eating meat that had been dedicated to idols (as most of the meat in the market had) was a sin and others did not. His answer was personal liberty but surrendered if necessary to avoid wounding other Christians. It is worth taking the time to read all of Romans chapter 14, but for convenience I will past a few extracts below.

> 1Accept the one whose faith is weak, without quarrelling over disputable matters. 2 One person's faith allows them to eat anything, but another, whose faith is weak, eats only vegetables. 3 The one who eats everything must not treat with contempt the one who does not, and the one who does not eat everything must not judge the one who does, for God has accepted them.

> 5 One person considers one day more sacred than another; another considers every day alike. Each of them should be fully convinced in their own mind. 6 Whoever regards one day as special does so to the Lord. Whoever eats meat does so to the Lord, for they give thanks to God; and whoever abstains does so to the Lord and gives thanks to God.

> 13 Therefore let us stop passing judgment on one another. Instead, make up your mind not to put any stumbling block or obstacle in the way of a brother or sister.

> 19 Let us therefore make every effort to do what leads to peace and to mutual edification. 20 Do not destroy the work of God for the sake of food. All food is clean, but it is wrong for a person to eat anything that causes someone else to stumble. 21 It is better not to eat meat or drink wine or to do anything else that will cause your brother or sister to fall.

The application to re-baptism I believe is this: firstly enjoy your liberty to believe what you believe, but do not judge other Christians who believe differently. Secondly be prepared to forego your own "rights" in order to avoid causing other Christians to stumble.

So if you are joining a denomination where re-baptism is required: do not make an issue of it. Certainly do not accept their doctrine that re-baptism is essential to being accepted by Christ - that way heresy lies! But do not make it into an issue yourself. If you want to join their church, be re-baptised and do it joyfully.

If you belong to a denomination which finds re-baptism offensive - do not deliberately offend them. I think I have said enough above to show that re-baptism is at the very least "disputable" so even if you believe it is a good thing, you can nonetheless with a clear conscience forego you right to it so as not to distract your brothers and sisters in Christ in your chosen denomination from concentrating on Jesus by making baptism a controversy. I once allowed a zealous Baptist laywoman help in our youth group (and she did many good things) but she got most of the young people - including some of my own children - re-baptised. For that I was (yet again) in serious trouble with the Archbishop - to him it was a matter of grave offence! So, consider others in what you do.

Believe in Jesus ... And ...

"You believe in Jesus ... Now you need to give up smoking/lose weight/join XYZ social action cause, etc." - Wrong!

I have lumped a few disparate issues together just to illustrate the sort of thing you may be exhorted to do as part of your new found faith. Don't fall for it for a moment! Remember what Paul said to the Christians in Galatia. Any one of these activities may be harmless in themselves, they may even be good things but the moment they become added as something necessary to complete your faith in Jesus they become spiritual poison.

Take smoking. Giving it up is sound medical advice, but it is not a matter of salvation. It may seem harmless to people to just add it in as an article of faith, but the spiritual effect of that is like putting carbon monoxide into the air we breathe.

A number of people I know found that not long after they came to faith the Holy Spirit laid it on them to give up their cigarette habit and the Holy Spirit gave them the strength and encouragement to do it. That is the sort of thing the Holy Spirit does in a believer's life as much as we will allow. But it is the Holy Spirit who decides what aspects of our life need changing and in what order. The Holy Spirit brings us around to agree to each change in turn and gives us the power to do it. For other humans to try to set the agenda for us is really not helpful.

With things like losing weight it is again a problem of doing the right thing for the wrong reason. On the personal level you might decide to do it for health reasons. That's fine. You may decide to do it for aesthetics. That's fine too (within reason of course). But being overweight is not a sin. Gluttony is the sin, where a person turns food into something they effectively worship.

> For, as I have often told you before and now tell you again even with tears, many live as enemies of the cross of Christ. Their destiny is destruction, their god is their stomach, and their glory is in their shame. Their mind is set on earthly things. (Philippians 3.18,19)

Being overweight may be one of the consequences of gluttony, but the aim of a Christian shouldn't be to lose weight, but to break our sinful attitude! Those who preach that you should lose weight are generally not trying to deal with the sin of making an idol of our appetites. Instead, they are trying to mix belief in "healthy living" - which is one of the false religions of our age - with faith in Jesus.

These additions are neither necessary for salvation, nor are they necessary for a holy, Christ-like life. The Holy Spirit may or may not convict you of some of these issues, and it is not for other people to demand that you work on this particular issue if the Holy Spirit is not strengthening you to do so. That is not to say Christians shouldn't promote good living. So let me illustrate this by wrong way/right way examples.

Right way: Suppose you are involved in some way in public health. Through this you have a concern that obesity is a widespread health problem. As a Christian you are even more interested in looking after people, so aided by the Holy Spirit you devise (let us say) a really effective anti-obesity program. It supports those who want to change, but does not condemn those who are not interested.

Wrong way: Same scenario down to being a Christian - you may or may not be. You are looking for ways of promoting your anti-obesity campaign (which we agree is a good thing) you come to see that bringing in religious sanctions will help motivate people. So your campaign says that not being overweight is necessary in order to be a good Christian.

Why is this wrong? Because you have (perhaps inadvertently) reduced saving faith in Jesus to being just the means to a thing you consider a "greater good" (public health in this case). This inevitably results in the greater "good" becoming the greater "god".

One last common form of this heresy is using Christianity as a means to promote XYZ cause, claiming that if you are Christian, you must support the cause. This is again a lie that can be mostly true (as the most effective lies are).

Along with adding to the Gospel, this heresy is dangerous because it can derail Christians from the path God wants them on. As you let God have a bigger and bigger say in your life, you find that he has PLANS. But his plans are tailor made for you, and something you will have great fun discovering and following in partnership with God. It may turn out that he wants you to be an activist changing the world, as William Wilberforce was. Or you may diligently and cheerfully do what people think is "just" an ordinary job such as being a bank clerk. In the process of faithfully fulfilling this role, you will be greatly pleasing God and perhaps spreading a little happiness to a lot of people. Similarly, you may stay home and raise children who turn out to love God and be well adjusted adults and in the process please God inordinately. And so I could go on but you get to idea.

To let someone firstly make you think that joining their cause is part of believing in Jesus and secondly possibly derail you from following the plans God has for you is a double disaster. There are many important causes out there, and many important roles. God requires people for all of them. So just because God has said something is important for one person, that does not mean he wants everyone to do it! The tragedy is that many churches today are well populated with people whose devotion to this cause or that cause has eclipsed their devotion to Christ. It is sad because they are now dysfunctional Christians, and may even cease being Christians at all.

I sometimes even think there are people whose 'god' IS their political cause be it climate change, socialism, fascism, or any other "...ism" and who are like parasites invading churches to utilise them and their people for their cause! This is a tragedy, because both sorts of people are turning whole churches aside from serving Christ to serving their merely human political platforms. It is also sad because while they are being driven by their own (or the world's) agenda rather than God's plan they will go off-track in trying to fix up this broken world and often end up being part of the problem instead of part of the solution.

They will try to recruit you. Resist! There is nothing more important than Jesus and nothing pleases him as much as walking humbly with him on the path he has chosen for you.

Creationism

"A Christian must believe 'science is bad' and 'the world was created in 6 (solar) days'." - Wrong!

This one is, unfortunately, very common especially in more evangelical and fundamentalist circles. It has two really bad results a) people outside the church rejecting Christianity (wrongly) believing it is anti-science and b) Christians in these churches being sidetracked from devotion to Christ alone into fighting for the "cause" of creation science etc. I am dealing with it here because of its danger as an addition to the Gospel, but at the same time I will comment on the false "Christianity vs. Science" dichotomy.

I grew up in a denomination which although it contained many devout and godly Christians had fallen into an "adding to the Gospel" trap with creationism (and also special foods and Sabbath). So I do have some first hand knowledge. I also remember vividly as a young teenager keenly interested in science what a put-off it was hearing science denounced from the pulpit, and how silly preachers sounded who railed at scientific things which they very obviously did not understand!

When I was studying for my High School finals, I was taking Geology as an extra science subject. One of my younger cousins, who still belonged to that denomination came into my room one day. As he saw me sitting there surrounded by geology textbooks his look turned to horror and he blurted out "But you do believe in God, don't you?"

So let me cover the "science is bad" fallacy in a few words first. This fallacy has been fed by atheists opposed to Christianity - from Darwin to Dawkins - who have tried to use science in their cause. In their desire to discredit Christianity, they have set up science in opposition to it. So what if they use science as a weapon? It is them not science that are anti-Christian. They do not understand Christianity or the purpose of religion, and although they might have knowledge of science, that doesn't make their conclusions correct!

It has also been fed by the more fundamentalist preachers who have bought into the atheists' lie that Christianity and science are trying to say the same thing but only one can be correct. They have fallen for this in two ways. Firstly they have not realised that the real answer to the atheist scientists' attacks is to remember that science deals with the question "how" while theology deals with the question "why". Neither has anything to fear from the other, and are not in opposition to each other in the search for truth. Secondly these preachers have very inadvisably tried to use Genesis as a science text book (I will deal more with that later). This is just agreeing with the atheists that Christianity is primarily interested in the same things science is, which God has never said.

What is modern science? It is a search for truth. It is a search for answers to the question "how?" in relation to this world. And modern science is the child of devout Christians of long ago who, because they believed God created everything and that God was dependable, believed that there would be a "rhyme and reason" to the world and so they confidently looked for it and discovered things like the 'laws' of physics. If you believe in a logical, orderly God it is reasonable to believe that his creation can be studied in a logical, orderly way. But note it is the study of his creation, not him.

So what is "bad" about science? Jesus said "I am the Truth" so searching for truth cannot be bad. This applies especially for us who believe God created everything. For us, discovering the "how" of his creation should be an exciting and noble thing. The scientific enterprise, scientific mindset and scientific method are things that we Christians should be thanking God for, not disavowing and most certainly not stigmatising as bad. The problem comes when you try to get science to do the job of theology, or theology to do the job of science, as one is how and one is why.

Back to creationism as an addition to the Gospel. You may have seen news clips of conflict in the United States at various times with people objecting violently to "evolution" being taught in schools and wanting "creationism" taught alongside it. The passion with which these people pursue their cause is testament to the importance they attach to it. In Australia you will find churches, and may even have joined such a church, that hold creationism with similar passion. They often argue that if you do not believe in Creationism, you do not believe in the Bible, and by extension therefore your faith in God is questioned. In this case it has changed from being a disputable matter in which a Christian can believe whatever they like to a heresy because it is pulling people away from devotion to Christ and making claims to salvation.

My aim here is most certainly not to get into an argument on the actual subject of "Creationism Vs Evolution". That is the very last thing I want to do. What I want to do is show that it is not an essential part of Christian belief, but rather a matter on which every Christian has freedom to hold whatever views they like. They should also extend that freedom to others. Especially I want to show that elevating it to an Article of Faith makes it into a heresy.

How do I show it is not an essential Christian belief? Here goes ...

When I was at theological college I had two very good Old Testament lecturers. One was Dr. Bill Dumbrell. He was a devout Christian (rare I am afraid in Biblical scholars) as well as being a formidable scholar. As an example of the type of scholar he was, at the start of a semester unit on "Genesis chapters 1 to 11" he started by dictating the names of good reference books which we slavishly wrote down. He seemed bemused that we all dropped our pens when, after one book he added what he obviously thought was a matter of no consequence: "It is several hundred pages ... in German". He was that sort of scholar!

Having a great respect for both his theological scholarship and his strong faith in Christ, I was interested in his answer when one lesson someone asked him if he believed the world was created in six days. He said that if he found that a sound interpretation of the Bible required that belief, then he would believe it without hesitation. But, in fact, he did not believe that the Bible said that. And he went on to talk about the way the Bible used the word "day" and other items which I won't digress on to here.

There are many great Christian scholars who have the same view, going back to Augustine in the fourth century A.D. I realise that his belief does not prove anything, but it does give us a good reason not to allow ourselves to be swept along by claims that the Bible "obviously" says the world was literally created in six solar days. If you hear someone say this, this should be a warning bell.

My next reason is to do with Gallileo. In 1633 Galileo was condemned to prison by a church Inquisition for the heresy of "holding as true the fallacy that the sun is at the centre ..."

Three hundred and sixty years later the reigning pope said this:

> Thanks to his intuition as a brilliant physicist and by relying on different arguments, Galileo, who practically invented the experimental method, understood why only the sun could function as the centre of the world, as it was then known, that is to say, as a planetary system. The error of the theologians of the time, when they maintained the centrality of the Earth, was to think that our understanding of the physical world's structure was, in some way, imposed by the literal sense of Sacred Scripture ...
>
> Pope John Paul II, *L'Osservatore Romano* N. 44 (1264) - November 4, 1992

So Galileo was condemned because the theologians of his time believed the Bible said that the earth was the centre of the universe and the sun went around the earth. I do not think any Christian today would believe the sun goes round the earth, but we still read the same passages out of the same Bible as those theologians did.

So when today we have scientists saying that the evidence appears to show that the world came to be in such and such a way we should be cautious about acting like the Inquisition of Galileo's day and declaring "No! It cannot be! The Bible says it happened in six days!" The Bible has important things to say about why the world around us is the way it is and why evil exists, what God has done about it and how we should live to please God. These are the things that really matter. So the Bible may not have the least interest in teaching spiritually unimportant things like the world's physical structure.

My last reason is in the answer to this question: "What difference would it make to our faith?"

I don't have any difficulty in believing God could create the universe in an instant let alone over six days. But what if the modern scientific theory is correct (and of course it may be supplanted by another theory any time); what changes in my appreciation of God?

Well, if I imagine God putting forth some stupendous burst of pure energy, bounding it I suppose by what we know as the laws of physics, watching for billions of years while nebulae, galaxies and solar systems form knowing that out of all this vast array of stars at least one will have a suitable planet for life. Perhaps he does or perhaps he does not kick start that first anaerobic life. (He may for all I know have set up the whole thing to run to produce his desired result without further intervention - that would be very clever indeed!) If I imagine him watching as this world is "polluted" by oxygen (a biologist called it the earth's greatest ecological disaster) and most life forms are killed off. Then as oxygen-based life flourishes he does or perhaps does not need to give it a push here and a shove there. Then as millions of years roll by he may or may not tweak things so that something recognisably human emerges. Perhaps there is indeed a first breeding pair who are "human" maybe he starts to talk to them and gives them a really simple test of obedience "don't eat the fruit of this tree" ...

I am no biologist and I may not have done the current theories of astronomy and evolution justice, but my point is that such an account is to me just as glorifying to God, and does not detract from any essential piece of doctrine that I know. It also does not mean that the Bible is false, only how some people have interpreted it.

Treating Genesis as a science textbook diverts attention away from the really fundamental doctrines it sets forth: how evil come into the world - we humans let it in; why we suffer natural disasters - because we humans decided to try to run the world instead of God; of God's kindness that despite what we did, God did not totally stop helping us; of the beginning of God's way of setting to rights what we humans had made wrong. These teachings are really important, and they are what Genesis is really about.

There is a justly famous principle of the English reformation: "In essentials, unity; in doubtful matters, liberty; in all things, charity." This principle is a very good one to apply to Creation Vs Evolution. The question of which is correct is not an essential of the Christian Faith, rather it is definitely a "doubtful matter" so the correct approach is liberty. Believe what you believe, but grant other Christians the same liberty to believe what they believe. That way you will avoid turning your pet belief into a heresy that harms your Christian life and growth.

As Paul wrote of a different but I think analogous situation: "But avoid foolish controversies and genealogies and arguments and quarrels about the law, because these are unprofitable and useless." (Titus 3.9)

CHAPTER SEVEN

Heresies of the Second Kind

Diluting The Gospel

The second kind of heresy comprises diluting the Gospel. Specifically it is mixing in bits from other religions or even secular philosophies. The technical name for it is "syncretism".

Syncretism was such a constant problem in the Old Testament that we should expect it to be continuing to happen now. And there is no reason to suspect that the Old Testament warnings about syncretistic practices and how much God hates them doesn't apply to us today too.

Before we look at modern examples, let's look at some from the Old Testament. It is one of the major themes throughout most of the Old Testament, but I will only give a few references here. In your reading of the Bible you will soon see how much of a problem it was.

> Again the Israelites did evil in the eyes of the LORD. They served the Baals and the Ashtoreths, and the gods of Aram, the gods of Sidon, the gods of Moab, the gods of the Ammonites and the gods of the Philistines. And because the Israelites forsook the LORD and no longer served him, he became angry with

them. He sold them into the hands of the Philistines and the Ammonites, who that year shattered and crushed them. For eighteen years they oppressed all the Israelites on the east side of the Jordan in Gilead, the land of the Amorites. The Ammonites also crossed the Jordan to fight against Judah, Benjamin and the house of Ephraim; and Israel was in great distress. Then the Israelites cried out to the LORD, "We have sinned against you, forsaking our God and serving the Baals."

The LORD replied, "When the Egyptians, the Amorites, the Ammonites, the Philistines, the Sidonians, the Amalekites and the Maonites oppressed you and you cried to me for help, did I not save you from their hands? But you have forsaken me and served other gods, so I will no longer save you. Go and cry out to the gods you have chosen. Let them save you when you are in trouble!"

But the Israelites said to the LORD, "We have sinned. Do with us whatever you think best, but please rescue us now." Then they got rid of the foreign gods among them and served the LORD. (Judges 10. 6-16)

The cult of the pagan gods would become so much a part village life and get so mixed up with the real worship of God that anyone opposing it risked death. When Gideon was chosen by God to rescue Israel the first task God set him was to destroy his village's pagan idols. It nearly cost him his life.

That same night the LORD said to him, "Take the second bull from your father's herd, the one seven years old. Tear down your father's altar to Baal and cut down the Asherah pole beside it. Then build a proper kind of altar to the LORD your God on the top of this height. Using the wood of the Asherah pole that you cut down, offer the second bull as a burnt offering."

So Gideon took ten of his servants and did as the LORD told him. But because he was afraid of his family and the townspeople, he did it at night rather than in the daytime.

In the morning when the people of the town got up, there was Baal's altar, demolished, with the Asherah pole beside it cut down and the second bull sacrificed on the newly built altar!

They asked each other, "Who did this?"

When they carefully investigated, they were told, "Gideon son of Joash did it."

The people of the town demanded of Joash, "Bring out your son. He must die, because he has broken down Baal's altar and cut down the Asherah pole beside it."

But Joash replied to the hostile crowd around him, "Are you going to plead Baal's cause? Are you trying to save him? Whoever fights for him shall be put to death by morning! If Baal really is a god, he can defend himself when someone breaks down his altar." So that day they gave Gideon the name Jerub-Baal, saying, "Let Baal contend with him," because he broke down Baal's altar. (Judges 6.25-32)

The problem continued over the centuries. Even when the people claimed they were worshipping God, they added pagan practices to their worship.

So do not pray for this people nor offer any plea or petition for them; do not plead with me, for I will not listen to you. Do you not see what they are doing in the towns of Judah and in the streets of Jerusalem? The children gather wood, the fathers light the fire, and the women knead the dough and make cakes to offer to the Queen of Heaven. They pour out drink offerings to other gods to arouse my anger. But am I the one they are provoking? declares the LORD. Are they not rather harming themselves, to their own shame?

Therefore this is what the Sovereign LORD says: My anger and my wrath will be poured out on this place - on people and animals, on the trees of the field and on the crops of your land - and it will burn and not be quenched.

This is what the LORD Almighty, the God of Israel, says: Go ahead, add your burnt offerings to your other sacrifices and eat the meat yourselves! For when I brought your ancestors out of Egypt and spoke to them, I did not just give them commands about burnt offerings and sacrifices, but I gave them this command: Obey me, and I will be your God and you will be my people. Walk in obedience to all I command you, that it may go well with you. But they did not listen or pay attention; instead, they followed the stubborn inclinations of their evil hearts. (Jeremiah 6.16-23)

This word came to Jeremiah concerning all the Jews living in Lower Egypt - in Migdol, Tahpanhes and Memphis - and in Upper Egypt: "This is what the LORD Almighty, the God of Israel, says: You saw the great disaster I brought on Jerusalem and on all the towns of Judah. Today they lie deserted and in ruins because of the evil they have done. They aroused my anger by burning incense to and worshipping other gods that neither they nor you nor your ancestors ever knew. Again and again I sent my servants the prophets, who said, 'Do not do this detestable thing that I hate!' But they did not listen or pay attention; they did not turn from their wickedness or stop burning incense to other gods. Therefore, my fierce anger was poured out; it raged against the towns of Judah and the streets of Jerusalem and made them the desolate ruins they are today."(Jeremiah 44. 1-6)

The destruction of Jerusalem we know for a historical fact. From the Bible we know that it came as a judgment from God after generations of disobedience by the people and in particular worshiping other gods, including the "queen of heaven". This act of God in history, among others, gives absolute certainty to the truth of his words through Jeremiah and other prophets that he really hates his people worshiping false gods. Yet they still do it to this day.

I visited Ephesus with a group during a tour of Turkey. As we sat in the ruins of the ancient amphitheater, our guide read out the passage in Acts 19 where there is a riot in Ephesus and a crowd gathered in the amphitheatre and for two hours shouted "great is Artemis of the Ephesians". The guide had previously been at pains to tell us that the Ephesian Artemis was quite different to the Greek one. The goddess they worshiped had a totally different (and rather repulsive) statue representation. He pointed out that the place had been the site of "mother-goddess" worship from almost prehistoric times, and the goddess had been successively re-badged: from an earth-mother-goddess, of which 6,000 year old figurines had been found, to the cult of Cybele then on to this distinctively Anatolian Artemis. Our tour notes, written by an Anglican theologian from Melbourne, also mentioned this and made the further connection that with the ascendance of Christianity the temple of Artemis was destroyed but that it was then in Ephesus that the cult of Mary worship began.

It seemed that whatever spiritual forces had been worshiped there over the millennia had again been re-badged, this time as "the virgin Mary", and had gotten itself added to Christian worship; just as Baal and Asherah worship had been added to the worship of God in ancient Israel.

As we traveled we found that this belief had invaded Christianity in many countries. We saw so many churches that had large statues in them, richly adorned, of a female figure wearing a crown. Supposedly they were statues of "the virgin Mary". We noticed that they were often titled the "queen of heaven". That title itself takes one back to Israel in Jeremiah's day where the people were worshiping a "queen of heaven" as well as God - and it made God so angry he destroyed them! We appear not to have learned the lesson.

In our hotel in Civitavecchia there was a booklet about a local jeweller. He was apparently famous for making richly adorned crowns for "queen of heaven" statues. Some of his crowns had even been blessed, the booklet said, by the Pope. I was terribly saddened to read this as it indicated that pagan idolatry was condoned and even given false legitimacy by people who should know much better.

Nothing could be less honouring to the memory of Jesus' earthly mother than these pagan goddess idols. Nothing could be less like following her own good example than the whole "Mary" cult.

The real Mary was a woman who loved God. Look at her response to the angel Gabriel. Told that she was to bear the long awaited Messiah, even though she was not having sex with her fiancée, she says simply "may it be as you have said". That is faith! Not just belief that God could do the "impossible" but also trusting that God would save her from the consequences. She would have been acutely aware of Joseph's (and the community's) likely reaction to hearing she was pregnant when he knew he had not had sex with her.

Then we read of that beautiful moment when Mary and Elizabeth are together. God's plan to save all humankind is about to break in on the world, and here are the two key women, the only ones who know - Mary who is to bear the Messiah and Elizabeth who is to bear John Baptist who will prepare the way for him - and these two women are filled with excitement and supporting each other. They are seen here as truly great women of God.

From there to the grief stricken mother at the foot of the cross and on to the Mary we are told in Acts was one of the worshiping community before the day of Pentecost. The real Mary was a woman of great faith in God. A woman who was there praying with the early believers soon after Jesus was raised from the dead. A woman who, as a devout Jew, would have thought it utterly wicked to worship or pray to anyone or anything other than the one true God.

To the real Mary this cult of "the blessed virgin Mary" would be utterly abhorrent. The real Mary would revile these "queen of heaven" statues as the pagan idols they really are.

One point I should perhaps add before I leave this subject. The Roman Empire, as you might know, accepted Christianity under Emperor Constantine who gained power in 306AD. Under him the seat of government moved from Rome to Constantinople (modern Istanbul). The empire was mostly Greek speaking in these eastern parts, but clung to Latin in the west. The Greek speaking part started using the term *theotokos* literally "god-bearer" for Mary. That was half right - she was the human being through whom Jesus who is both God and Human was born. But she had only to do with the human side of the equation. Jesus was God before the world was created and came into his creation through the power of the Holy Spirit in his conception.

As the Bible says in Romans 1.2-4:

> The gospel he promised beforehand through his prophets in the Holy Scriptures regarding his Son, who as to his earthly life was a descendant of David, and

who through the Spirit of holiness was appointed the Son of God in power by his resurrection from the dead: Jesus Christ our Lord.

As to his humanity, Mary was Jesus' mother because she was human, but not in respect to his divine nature.

As Jesus himself said in John 10.36 "what about the one whom the Father set apart as his very own and sent into the world? Why then do you accuse me of blasphemy because I said, 'I am God's Son'?."

In John 8 Jesus stresses his pre-existence: "Very truly I tell you," Jesus answered, "before Abraham was born, I am!"

And remember the wonderful beginning of John's Gospel where he says about Jesus:

In the beginning was the Word, and the Word was with God, and the Word was God. He was with God in the beginning. Through him all things were made; without him nothing was made that has been made.

Jesus was "God-the-Son" before Mary was born, before Abraham was born, before the universe was created, before even time existed.

So even using the term *theotokos* "god-bearer" was really shaky ground. When the term moved to the Latin speaking west it lost something in the translation and became even more inaccurate: "mother of god". This is wholly false! God, Father, Son and Holy Spirit is eternal and has no mother! Mary was a human being: a devout and faithful human being, but just a human being; a very important human being in God's plans, but just a human being; a human being who was very dear to Jesus, but just a human being.

So, do not be deceived into this idolatry no matter how cleverly it proponents try to camouflage it or "explain" it to you.

Remember that any teaching that requires you to dilute the Gospel, adding in elements into Christian worship from other religions, is insulting to God. In the Old Testament God set up the covenant with the people based on a one-on-one relationship: I will be their God and they will be my people. You have entered into this covenant, so don't now try to include anything else. There will be teachers who tell you that God doesn't really mean all the exclusivity stuff, and wants you to embrace other religions and practices. If you know your Old Testament, you know that nothing could be further from the truth! God loves all people, not all practices!

CHAPTER EIGHT

Heresies of the Third Kind

Indulging The Flesh

Perhaps I should have made these the "first kind" because the serpent in the garden of Eden used this approach to tempt our first parents into disobeying God. His two pronged attack was: 1. "you will not die" when God had warned them "Touch and die!" 2. He lied to them saying it would give them desirable things - in that case knowledge to be like God. After umpteen generations of fallen human nature trying to drag us back from God, this sort of heresy is a really potent killer!

Yes indeed! These are a really tempting ones. The Bible talks about us having to "put to death" our old human nature and all its desires. That sounds painful. That is painful. Our old human nature puts up a strong fight. Our old human nature will do almost anything to survive. So the possibility of a "Christianity" that allows our old human nature to run our lives is going to be very, very appealing. Appealing though it certainly is, the Bible says plainly and often that it is also a "Christianity" that will certainly land you in hell.

Let us take this one a step at a time. First: dying to our old self.

This book began with the baptismal promises which included renouncing "the devil and all his works, the vain pomp and glory of the world, with all covetous desires of the same, and the carnal desires of the flesh". This is a concise statement of what the Bible teaches from one end to the other. Here are just a few New Testament passages.

In Matthew 16.24-27:

> Then Jesus said to his disciples, "Whoever wants to be my disciple must deny themselves and take up their cross and follow me. For whoever wants to save their life will lose it, but whoever loses their life for me will find it. What good will it be for you to gain the whole world, yet forfeit your soul? Or what can you give in exchange for your soul? For the Son of Man is going to come in his Father's glory with his angels, and then he will reward everyone according to what they have done."

Romans chapters 6, 7 and 8 are devoted to this theme and I encourage you to read the whole of it. Here are just two slices:

> In the same way, count yourselves dead to sin but alive to God in Christ Jesus. Therefore do not let sin reign in your mortal body so that you obey its evil desires. Do not offer any part of yourself to sin as an instrument of wickedness, but rather offer yourselves to God as those who have been brought from death to life; and offer every part of yourself to him. (Romans 6.11-13)

> Therefore, brothers and sisters, we have an obligation—but it is not to the sinful nature, to live according to it. For if you live according to the sinful

nature, you will die; but if by the Spirit you put to death the misdeeds of the body, you will live. (Romans 8.12,13)

Galatians 5 is another whole section dealing with this theme. Here are a few verses (16-24):

So I say, walk by the Spirit, and you will not gratify the desires of the sinful nature. For the sinful nature desires what is contrary to the Spirit, and the Spirit what is contrary to the sinful nature. They are in conflict with each other, so that you are not to do whatever you want. But if you are led by the Spirit, you are not under the law.

The acts of the sinful nature are obvious: sexual immorality, impurity and debauchery; idolatry and witchcraft; hatred, discord, jealousy, fits of rage, selfish ambition, dissensions, factions and envy; drunkenness, orgies, and the like. I warn you, as I did before, that those who live like this will not inherit the kingdom of God.

But the fruit of the Spirit is love, joy, peace, patience, kindness, goodness, faithfulness, gentleness and self-control. Against such things there is no law. Those who belong to Christ Jesus have crucified the sinful nature with its passions and desires.

2 Peter 2 is yet another chapter worth careful study. Here are some verses (1-3, 18-21):

But there were also false prophets among the people, just as there will be false teachers among you. They will secretly introduce destructive heresies, even denying the sovereign Lord who bought them - bringing swift destruction on themselves. Many will follow their depraved conduct and will bring the way of truth into disrepute. In their greed these teachers will exploit you with fabricated stories.

For they mouth empty, boastful words and, by appealing to the lustful desires of sinful human nature, they entice people who are just escaping from those who live in error. They promise them freedom, while they themselves are slaves of depravity - for "people are slaves to whatever has mastered them." If they have escaped the corruption of the world by knowing our Lord and Saviour Jesus Christ and are again entangled in it and are overcome, they are worse off at the end than they were at the beginning. It would have been better for them not to have known the way of righteousness, than to have known it and then to turn their backs on the sacred command that was passed on to them.

These are strong and frightening words. Notice that Peter sees that the power of these heresies is that they appeal to the lustful desires of sinful human nature. I will end this part with Jesus's warning about the ultimate fate of those who follow these false teachings:

Not everyone who says to me, 'Lord, Lord,' will enter the kingdom of heaven, but only those who do the will of my Father who is in heaven. Many will say to me on that day, 'Lord, Lord, did we not prophesy in your name and in your name drive out demons and in your name perform many miracles?' Then I will tell them plainly, 'I never knew you. Away from me, you evildoers!' (Matthew 7.21-23)

Next, what are some modern versions of this false teaching?

Faith Heals All Diseases

"Have Faith and God Will Heal ALL Your Diseases" - Wrong!

This is a truth taken to the extreme where it becomes a lie. God can and does work miracles. You won't read too far in the Bible without discovering that. What he does not do is cure every disease of every Christian "if they have enough faith". This should be obvious, because ever since Christ's resurrection, everyone else has still had a physical death from one means or another.

Let me first say that I am not denying that God does heal. What I am arguing against is the teaching that all believers should be healthy and pain-free all the time, that if you are sick and continue to be sick after someone has prayed for you, it is because you are not faithful enough. This is dangerous because it focuses on our personal comfort over God.

This heresy is part of what is sometimes called "over-realized eschatology" which is theologian-speak for thinking we have here and now things which the Bible promises we will enjoy in heaven. Yes, in heaven we will all be healed eg Rev.21.4 "He will wipe every tear from their eyes. There will be no more death or mourning or crying or pain, for the old order of things has passed away." Yes, God does do miracles even now to authenticate the message about Jesus and to give us little flashes of heaven. But no, he does not heal every Christian - we are still in this world and it is a world marred by sin, suffering and death.

Let me illustrate some of the pain this heresy causes from some of my own experiences as a priest.

Many years ago I was visiting patients in the tiny country hospital in my parish when I and everyone else heard a zealous Pentecostal pastor shouting "In the name of Jesus you are healed!" to a woman dying of cancer. She died some weeks later. But fearful of losing her "healing" by exhibiting lack of faith she refused any pain relief. She still died, but she died in terrible pain. I heard that the Pentecostal pastor explained her death away to his congregation by saying she didn't have enough faith to be healed.

About the same time there was a world famous Anglican charismatic leader Rev. David Watson. He was stricken with cancer. Believers all over the world were praying for his healing. He died. Without missing a beat the Pentecostal spin doctors announced that "obviously" he was not healed because he didn't really want healing.

It struck me with these and other cases that the people who put out this heresy were simply not honest. Suppose a scientist says: "If my theory is true, 'X' will happen" Now suppose 'X' does not happen. The scientist will say "my theory is wrong". No matter how much he had invested in that theory being right (maybe years of work and the prospect of fame, fortune and even a Nobel Prize) a true scientist would publish the real results and say "my theory was wrong".

Perversely these people said "you are healed" but when this did not happen even in the clearest way possible - that is by the person dying - they still clung fanatically to their now disproved "theory" and invented spin to cover up the truth!

So my experience was that this doctrine caused great harm. Also because it dealt in lies, it was of the devil, not of God. My experience has also been that once a believer has been hooked on this teaching nothing can rescue them.

There is a saying, "reality bites". They can shout all they like and claim with total conviction that a person is healed but if the person then dies of the disease that was supposedly healed then reality has "bitten". What they claimed was not really true at all. Jesus said, "I am the Truth ..." and also "the devil is a liar and the father of all lies" So however much these healers take the name of Jesus on their lips, they are actually doing the work of the devil.

Yes, since we long for heaven we would love to have its joys right now. So, yes we would love to believe this doctrine and believe the evangelists who spread it. But it is always better for a person to act on a painful truth than to believe and act on a comfortable falsehood!

Most importantly this teaching like the other heresies is spiritual carbon-monoxide. Our old human nature really wants "religion" that gives health and prosperity. So these teachings that God will heal every disease once we learn the secrets of "faith" to make him do it is one our sinful nature will grab with both hands.

I have not yet trotted out Bible verses for a very good reason. This teaching is a truth taken to an extreme where it becomes a lie. So if the false teacher says, "the Old Testament has lots of miraculous healings." I say, "True, it does and I believe they really happened." When the false teacher says, "Jesus healed all kinds of diseases and even raised dead people to life," I agree. He did. When he or she continues, "And God did great miracles through the Apostles like Peter and Paul." I say again, "I too believe those accounts in the Bible are true." When they play their trump card and say, "And God still does miracles today," I say, "Yes indeed, I too have seen many miraculous answers to prayer. I have seen enough genuine miracles to believe beyond doubt that God still does miracles today."

So most of what these faith healers preach, I believe is true. But it only takes a tiny bit of poison added to a healthy meal to kill you. The poison in their otherwise true teaching is in three parts:

1. It is a false, worldly view of the Christian life. Jesus never promised a bed of roses (in this life anyway).

2. It is a false "faith". They turn the real and precious attitude of devotion, trust and unshakeable reliance on Jesus into a mind game which soon crosses over into shamanism.

3. It makes a basic error of logic. They confuse God being the same "yesterday, today and forever" with God acting the same when circumstances change. Big mistake!

Lets look at these in a bit more detail:

a) Jesus didn't promise a bed of roses. Quite the opposite: he made it clear that becoming his follower was the hard choice, that there was a cost, that some believers would fall away when they realised this. He warned of hardships and persecutions in this life, but glory in the world to come. Take the Parable of the Sower (Matthew 13) where he warned that some believers would fall away when they found it was hard going. He would not have warned that if he was promising them a trouble free life if they followed him. Another parable was the builder who didn't figure out the cost before he started (Luke 14.28). Read and think about it for yourself. Jesus is not talking home economics, he is talking about people deciding to be his followers. He is warning them that there is a cost. In this life the easy way is to ignore Jesus. Following him is harder (in this world) - so would-be followers should count the cost up-front. Once again Jesus would not say this if he was offering to magic away all life's problems. He never promised that!

The rest of the New Testament is dotted with statements to the effect that while the Christian life is hard now, the heavenly reward far outweighs the cost, and Christ is with us through all our trials and suffering. I will give just a few examples.

> I once thought these things were valuable, but now I consider them worthless because of what Christ has done. Yes, everything else is worthless when compared with the infinite value of knowing Christ Jesus my Lord. For his sake I have discarded everything else, counting it all as garbage, so that I could gain Christ and become one with him. (Philippians 3.7-9)

The point I wanted to draw from this was that happiness in this life was not the be all and end all, almost the reverse: for Paul all that counts is the joy of knowing Christ as saviour.

> In all this you greatly rejoice, though now for a little while you may have had to suffer grief in all kinds of trials. These have come so that your faith - of greater worth than gold, which perishes even though refined by fire - may be proved genuine and may result in praise, glory and honour when Jesus Christ is revealed. (1 Peter 1.6,7)

> All praise to God, the Father of our Lord Jesus Christ. God is our merciful Father and the source of all comfort. He comforts us in all our troubles so that we can comfort others. When they are troubled, we will be able to give them the same comfort God has given us. (2 Corinthians 1.3,4)

These verses were to comfort Christians going through trials and troubles. For Peter the pain is outweighed by the eternal benefit of a faith that has stood the test. For Paul writing to the Christians in Corinth it was that God comforts us in our trials rather than magic-ing them away, and we in turn can comfort others. The common point is that God does not always rescue us from suffering in this life.

The false teacher will say: "Ah, they are only talking about persecution, it does not apply to disease." Well, lets look at what Paul says to do when Timothy is ill. Does he recommend Timothy have more faith and he will become better? No. Paul says, "stop drinking only water, and use a little wine because of your stomach and your frequent illnesses." (1 Timothy 5.23). The New Testament writers are completely practical when it comes to normal illnesses. Further, Paul explicitly mentions an instance where he prays for healing, and God refuses to grant it to him.

> Therefore, in order to keep me from becoming conceited, I was given a thorn in my flesh, a messenger of Satan, to torment me. Three times I pleaded with the Lord to take it away from me. But he said to me, "My grace is sufficient for you, for my power is made perfect in weakness." Therefore I will boast all the more gladly about my weaknesses, so that Christ's power may rest on me. That is why, for Christ's sake, I delight in weaknesses, in insults, in hardships, in persecutions, in difficulties. For when I am weak, then I am strong. (2 Corinthians 12.7-10).

It is a much stronger testament to God what we persevere in weakness than that he takes all hardship away.

b) Faith is really basic to Christianity. Abraham is the prime example in the Bible of faith "because he believed God". Interestingly Genesis depicts Abraham warts and all and he had as many of those as most people. He wavered, he doubted, he did silly things, he even laughed when God said he would have a son by Sarah. You might say he just clung on to believing by his teeth - but the Bible gives him top marks. Jesus is often calling his disciples "little-faiths" but he persevered with them. Most of them ran away when he was arrested, and Peter swore he didn't know Jesus three times - but they go on to be the Apostles. Jesus told them that if they had faith as big as a mustard seed they could move mountains. I think the point he was making, and I am trying to make here is that even a little bit of faith counts a whole lot with God. He will of course want to train us to have a whole lot more over our lifetime, but for a start the teeniest bit will get us going. The faith healer uses faith in a totally different, and I believe wrong way, and runs the risk of blinding people to what real faith in Christ actually is.

The Bible gives some other examples of great faith. Hebrews 11 is a good example. It lists as heroes of faith with equal praise for people who had the faith to be miraculously delivered and people who had faith to keep trusting in God even when there was no miraculous deliverance. This puts the lie to the "faith healer"s excuse that people "didn't have enough faith to be healed". No, the Bible indicates it takes every bit as much faith not to have a miraculous deliverance from suffering and still hold fast to God.

How much more do I need to say? It would take too long to recount the stories of the faith of Gideon, Barak, Samson, Jephthah, David, Samuel, and all the prophets. By faith these people overthrew kingdoms, ruled with justice, and received what God had promised them. They shut the mouths of lions, quenched the flames of fire, and escaped death by the edge of the sword. Their weakness was turned to strength. They became strong in battle and put whole armies to flight. Women received their loved ones back again from death.

But others were tortured, refusing to turn from God in order to be set free. They placed their hope in a better life after the resurrection. Some were jeered at, and their backs were cut open with whips. Others were chained in prisons. Some died by stoning, some were sawed in half, and others were killed with the sword. Some went about wearing skins of sheep and goats, destitute and oppressed and mistreated. They were too good for this world, wandering over deserts and mountains, hiding in caves and holes in the ground.

All these people earned a good reputation because of their faith. (Hebrews 11.32-39)

c) The faith healer frequently recounts the miracles of Jesus, stresses with great literalness that he "healed all the sick" (eg Matthew 8.16), then quotes the text "Jesus Christ the same yesterday today and forever" (Hebrews 13.8) and jumps to the conclusion "therefore Jesus will heal all the sick today!"

That is a false conclusion. The result of Jesus being unchanging in his nature is that he will in fact respond differently in different situations.

Let me illustrate it this way. Think of a teacher marking multiple choice exam papers - you know the sort where for each question you answer by circling (a), (b), (c) etc on the exam paper. Suppose the correct answers are (a) for question 1. (b) for question 2. and (c) for question 3.

The teacher should mark every student who circled (a) for question 1 "correct" and every student who marked anything else for question 1 "wrong". And so forth down all the questions. To put this in the language we were using about Jesus - the teacher uses the same list of right answers to mark every paper in that exam.

So why do some students get good results and some get bad results?

The answer is obvious: some students knew their subject and marked lots of the correct answers and some students didn't know their work and marked lots of incorrect answers. The teacher's marking was the same for all students: he or she awarded good marks to good students and bad marks to bad students.

In the Bible there are enough examples of God maintaining an unchanging attitude, but changing his actions because people changed their ways. For example, Jonah is sent to Nineveh to tell them God is going to destroy the city because they are so wicked. They repent and stop being evil. God relents and does not destroy them (much to Jonah's annoyance). God stayed the same, so when the situation changed his response to it changed too.

Jesus is the same "yesterday today and forever". Yes, but if the situation today is different then precisely because he remains dependably the same, he will respond differently.

When he was walking by the shores of Lake Galilee, Jesus was claiming to uniquely speak for God. He even said, "the very works that I am doing testify that the Father has sent me." (John 5.36). So miracles were his authentication.

If we are preaching Jesus to people who do not believe and God judges that miracles will likewise authenticate our message, then indeed we would expect God to work them. If we are not preaching Jesus where the message needs authentication, but would like some miracles for some other reason (to big note ourselves or our church for instance) then it is not the same situation and we should not expect him to work exactly the same way.

The crux of the problem is that they are telling people to expect (and demand of God even) what God promises we will enjoy in heaven, not here on earth. Certainly he gives little foretastes of it now just to encourage his people to set their hopes on Jesus and of being with him in heaven. God is always surprising us by his kindness, goodness and generosity. He is an incredibly wonderful being! Also he sometimes gives a sustained burst of spectacular miracles when he judges it necessary in order to authenticate his message. But to tell people that Jesus will heal every believer every time is wrong! It also has two really, really bad consequences. First it sets them up for the devil to pull the rug from under them and cause them to lose their faith in Jesus. Second it focuses them on themselves and their health and their comfort in this world - that keeps them as spiritual infants and mere worldlings. Grow up!

Yet if you ask, "But should we pray for healing?" My answer is, "Yes. It is part of our relationship with God that we can safely ask him for anything." As it says in 1 Peter 6.6,7 "Humble yourselves, therefore, under God's mighty hand, that he may lift you up in due time. Cast all your anxiety on him because he cares for you." Just don't believe the lie that if you are not healed, you don't have enough faith!

Prosperity Doctrine

"Jesus Wants to Make You Rich!" - Wrong!

How could anyone fall for this lie! Yet they do - and make shipwrecks of their faith!

I saw some time ago a TV documentary about some Christian churches in Nigeria. I found it terribly sad for the ordinary church members because they were being so cleverly and ruthlessly deceived by their leaders. The "gospel" they were taught was dominated by the themes of God making you healthy and God making you rich. I've already discussed the problems with believing God will always heal you. Believing that God will always give you riches is similar, and is really bad for three reasons.

1) It is spiritual carbon-monoxide pushing out the vital oxygen of the Gospel of reconciliation with God through Jesus by the forgiveness of our sins. If we give in and focus on it we will at the same time let go of Jesus and fall back into the world he was saving us from. As Peter said in the quote a while back: we are then worse off than if we had never known Jesus!

2) It is telling lies about God. It suggests God will magically turn up money for you or allow you to make it in ways other than by hard work. God does not create wealth by magic but in accordance with his decrees "by the sweat of your brow ..." and he does not encourage us to rob others, "I the Lord hate robbery and wrong".

3) For many of us, money is like an addiction, we handle it badly and always want more. God will not enable us to continue in this disfunction. For those who cannot handle a little, they should not expect God to give them alot.

Lets look at these more closely.

Our old poison gas ... carbon-monoxide. Let me say it again: the real Gospel is about how God reconciles humans to himself in Christ Jesus. All who come to him through his Son Jesus are forgiven, redeemed and adopted as children of God. In this life we get to be part of the "family business" - carrying on the work of Jesus. In the life-to-come we get heaven, forever, with God. Nothing could be more wonderful, more vital to be sought after, more to be prized than this!

Ah, but our old sinful nature wants the so called pleasures of this life! The Bible tells us plainly that if, by God's Holy Spirit we put to death this old human nature, we will live! If we live to please our sinful nature, we will die! So when the Devil's moles in the Church of God teach "God will make you rich" our sinful nature grabs that with both hands! That false gospel which leads to death is far more attractive to our sinful nature than the real one that leads to life. Just as carbon-monoxide is far more attractive to our red blood cells that life-giving oxygen.

What did Jesus say:

"It is easier for a camel to pass through the eye of a needle than for a rich person to enter the kingdom of heaven." (Matt 19.24)

"You cannot serve both God and money." (Matt 6.24)

"Do not store up for yourselves treasure on earth ... but store up treasure in heaven. For where your treasure is, there will your heart be also." (Matt. 6.19-21)

"The seed falling among the thorns refers to someone who hears the word, but the worries of this life and the deceitfulness of wealth choke the word, making it unfruitful". (Matt. 13.22 Parable of the Seeds)

Luke observes:

"The Pharisees, who loved money, heard all this and were sneering at Jesus." (Luke 16.14)

Paul wrote of the qualifications for a church leader: " ... not given to drunkenness, not violent but gentle, not quarrelsome, not a lover of money." (1 Timothy 3.3)

James wrote:

> Now listen, you rich people, weep and wail because of the misery that is coming on you. Your wealth has

rotted, and moths have eaten your clothes. Your gold and silver are corroded. Their corrosion will testify against you and eat your flesh like fire. You have hoarded wealth in the last days." (James 5.1-3)

Perhaps the most pointed teaching on the love of money is this:

> These are the things you are to teach and insist on. If anyone teaches otherwise and does not agree to the sound instruction of our Lord Jesus Christ and to godly teaching, they are conceited and understand nothing. They have an unhealthy interest in controversies and quarrels about words that result in envy, strife, malicious talk, evil suspicions and constant friction between people of corrupt mind, who have been robbed of the truth and who think that godliness is a means to financial gain.
>
> But godliness with contentment is great gain. For we brought nothing into the world, and we can take nothing out of it. But if we have food and clothing, we will be content with that. Those who want to get rich fall into temptation and a trap and into many foolish and harmful desires that plunge people into ruin and destruction. For the love of money is a root of all kinds of evil. Some people, eager for money, have wandered from the faith and pierced themselves with many griefs. (1 Timothy 6.2-10)

That does not exhaust the Bible's teaching on love of worldly wealth, but I hope those few quotes are sufficient for the moment to warn you against this false teaching. Focus on Christ and the Gospel, because to focus on prosperity can destroy your faith and let you fall into temptation. Do not believe anyone that says prosperity is a sign of your salvation, the Bible verses above alone should show you the problem with that.

The second argument against this teaching is that it suggests God will give you riches for no work or allow you to bend the rules to make it, if it's being used for a good cause of course. God does not 'magic' us money! His command back in Genesis 3 was "By the sweat of your brow ...". The legitimate way for us to get food, shelter, clothing is to work for it! So the legitimate way to become rich is to produce things through hard work. For a really good description of this read Proverbs 31.

Now when a person gives their life to Christ a lot of their former attitudes change. One consequence of this may well be that they are more diligent in their work and so prosper. Putting God first in their lives may spill over into them making more prudent decisions in all aspects of their life, so they may build rather than squander their money. For a host of reasons like this it may look that people who have become Christians prospered financially. But if they are real Christians they would gladly lose everything they own rather than lose Christ: Jesus not their money is their real treasure!

God hates thieving. He hates sharp business practices. He hates the rich swindling the poor. So "Christian" business people who think God will condone let alone assist them make money in any of these ways have a very wrong idea of God's holy character. They are in really serious danger of hearing him say, "get out of my sight I never knew you!" at the Judgment! (Matt. 7:23)

Just check out a few of the things God said about this behaviour:

> What shall I say about the homes of the wicked
>   filled with treasures gained by cheating?
> What about the disgusting practice
>   of measuring out grain with dishonest measures?

How can I tolerate your merchants
 who use dishonest scales and weights?
The rich among you have become wealthy
 through extortion and violence.
Your citizens are so used to lying
 that their tongues can no longer tell the truth.
(Micah 6.10-12 *New Living Translation*)

How you hate honest judges!
 How you despise people who tell the truth!
You trample the poor,
 stealing their grain through taxes and unfair rent.
Therefore, though you build beautiful stone houses,
 you will never live in them.
Though you plant lush vineyards,
 you will never drink wine from them.
For I know the vast number of your sins
 and the depth of your rebellions.
You oppress good people by taking bribes
 and deprive the poor of justice in the courts.
(Amos 5.10-12 *New Living Translation*)

Having read just a tiny bit of what the Bible has to say on this matter consider what was going on in some Nigerian churches. Nigeria has a per capita GDP less than one twenty-fifth that of Australia. So what sort of car would the head minister of a big church have in Nigeria? One they interviewed proudly showed his cars - a new Range Rover, a new Bentley and a Hummer - all high end luxury cars. He preached that God would make people in his congregation rich - provided of course they gave lots of money to him their minister!

There was, and may still be, a particularly nasty scam called "pyramid selling". When you cut through the clever sales pitch the scam amounted to this: people joining the money making scheme bought a worthless article from someone who had joined it before them for a large amount of money, with the promise that they could sell a number of these valueless things to the next layer of people they recruited to join the scheme. Of course the people at the top of this pyramid made a fortune. The bottom layer, those who joined the scheme just before it collapsed, all lost their money.

Well, these ministers seem to me to just be running a version of this scam: the few people at the top tell the large number of people below that they can become rich by handing up their money. The ones at or near the top of the pile do get rich - by defrauding the gullible people at the bottom who lose their money! The leaders do have houses and garages "filled with treasures gained by cheating" as God said through Micah. If the Bible is true, will they escape destruction?

So recognise this prosperity teaching for what it is: a dishonest way for church leaders who have become corrupt and lost touch with God to make money. Don't be a sucker! Especially don't become crooked like them!

The third argument deals with the wrong belief that all Christians should be enjoying God's prosperity. There are a number of reasons why Christians may have few or no possessions. On the one hand, strong and faithful Christians may have given up their worldly possessions in order to better serve Christ, or suffered financial persecution because of their faith. On the other hand, weak and growing Christians may also have little wealth because they are not good stewards of what they have been given, or not learnt to work appropriately.

The problem is, this heresy appeals most to those who are the least qualified to receive God's blessing of wealth! I was at a conference some years ago where a pentecostal laymen explained this problem. I mention that he was pentecostal because that is the section of the Church of God that is most infected with the prosperity doctrine. Also significant is that this man had a very large income.

His reason flowed from Jesus' teaching, particularly Luke 16:11 "So if you have not been trustworthy in handling worldly wealth, who will trust you with true riches?" He said that according to Jesus we were what would be called now "fiduciaries" for our worldly wealth and possessions. That is to say they are under our control, but they don't actually belong to us and so we have a duty to use them according to the wishes of the real owner. For us that real owner is Jesus - we were bought (as Peter wrote) "not with perishable things such as silver or gold ... but with the precious blood of Christ." Jesus owns us! So all our possessions are really owned by him. We need to learn to live this way on earth for our eternal good in heaven.

Those who teach the prosperity doctrine are usually telling it to those who are in debt and struggle managing the money they have. If you are not being faithful with the little you have, how can you expect God to give you more?

No good parent of a recovering alcoholic would give them alcohol. God as a perfect parent should not give wealth to any of his children who are money-addicts. On the other hand, those who have shown they can handle money as his fiduciaries in a small way may be trusted with handling more, even in this world.

So if you look at other Christians and see that they are being financially blessed, don't see that as a guarantee all Christians will be blessed. Instead, wealth can be a test for how each individual will handle what they are given. You just have to try and be as faithful as you can with what you have already received and trust God for the rest.

There are many other forms of this third kind of heresy, but when you step back they are generally recognisable by their appeal to the human flesh to the detriment of the Gospel. Yes, God does promise us life to the full and does want to bless his children. However, he also wants us to grow and develop in our trust in him, which often requires breaking our addiction to the old self. Therefore, if you come across a teaching that promises worldly comforts regardless of where you are at in your walk with Christ, be very wary. In the next section we will look at what to do if you find yourself in a church given to one of these heresies, and how to tell if it is serious.

PART FOUR

ABOUT CHURCH CONGREGATIONS

CHAPTER NINE

Recognising Different Churches

The Life-Cycle of Churches

This part is the practical application of what I have covered so far to your local congregation and the group of congregations to which it is linked.

There are some churches that do have serious problems. Some will be infected with one of the heresies I have discussed to the extent that it is spiritually dangerous. If you go to one of those you will have to take care not to become infected yourself. As long as you can keep yourself from absorbing that heresy God might want you to stay part of the church for other reasons. Remember that this side of heaven there is no such thing as a perfect church.

Others may in fact be harmful to an extent that you ought to leave.

Sometimes a church was at one time thriving, growing and effective for God. Then somewhere along the line they have taken the wrong road. In any one of a multitude of possible ways they have followed the dictates of sinful human nature instead of obeying Christ. So even if your church has a great history, don't be afraid to evaluate it as it now stands. If you can understand the lifecycle pattern of churches, it will be easier to identify if your church is starting to get into trouble.

I read a book on sociology of religion once that described a lifecycle common for churches in the U.S. It included a phase where formalism replaces vitality, bureaucracy increases and perpetuates its own interests, and the institution becomes the master instead of the servant of the members. This progresses to mimicking the non-believing society around it. Activities once considered secular proliferate as the church tries to become the centre of community. Sermons become topical lectures on social issues rather than dealing with sin and salvation.

Sometimes a reform group is able to rescue the church and renew its vitality and usefulness. Sometimes the reformers split from the church. Often they form a new church, which starts off (sociologically) looking like a sect, and then itself moves through the lifecycle stages over the next few generations.

Different heresies can appeal at the different life stages of a church. Often in the initial stages where there is vitality, people are passionate and this can lead to adding to the Gospel. For example they might have come together because they share a common interest in a cause which they add onto the Gospel. Or they might be trying to differentiate themselves from the dead churches they are leaving, so include an extra element as "protection" against becoming like that.

In the church building phases, they can also try to gain more members by promising healing and prosperity, to attract those who are turned off by the harder teachings of Christ. When churches start to become more formalised, heresies about having to do it 'our way' can become more common. They see the success that God has given them, and place it down to a particular thing that they have done. They may also start diluting the Gospel to make it more acceptable in the community, to cause less controversy by following local practices and customs.

I have also seen cases where people have let their church "brand" become an idol: their motivation has changed from doing things because they are pleasing to God to doing things so that their church will survive or grow big or become famous.

Another dysfunctional church type is where the minister or "the leadership" (if people talk about "the leadership" of their church with too much reverence, treat it as a danger signal!) become control freaks. Remember the quote "In essentials unity; in non-essentials liberty; in all things charity." Well, these churches allow no "liberty" and soon "charity" or Christian love is strictly reserved for those who slavishly obey The Leadership. Yes, there really are churches like that! They will seem friendly, welcoming, even kind and loving at first - but you will begin to see that this is conditional on you doing, thinking and believing everything you are told. Get out while you can! Your devotion and obedience belongs to God, not to any human. We humans, even the best intentioned of us, are all fallible sinners!

Types of Authority

While there are churches and ministers who are misled and misleading congregations, the Bible, of course, does not encourage us to be rebels. There is a proper spiritual authority which we should obey, but the point is there are limits to it. As a silly example, school children are expected to obey their teachers -

but not if the teacher tells them to rob a bank! That is the sort of thing we are talking about here - knowing the look and limits of genuine authority.

The sort of authority we should be respectful of is like this:

> Obey those who rule over you, and be submissive, for they watch out for your souls, as those who must give account. Let them do so with joy and not with grief, for that would be unprofitable for you. (Hebrews 13.17)

These good sort of ministers are trying to care for you knowing that one day they will have to answer to Jesus for how they looked after every one of the people Jesus entrusted to their care. The Bible often uses the analogy of sheep and shepherds. Only Jesus is "the Good Shepherd", but ministers are characterised as a sort of "junior shepherds" answerable to him.

In Acts 20.28-31 Paul exhorts the elders of the church in Ephesus:

> Keep watch over yourselves and all the flock of which the Holy Spirit has made you overseers. Be shepherds of the church of God, which he bought with his own blood. I know that after I leave, savage wolves will come in among you and will not spare the flock. Even from your own number some will arise and distort the truth in order to draw away disciples after them. So be on your guard!

Just as naughty and rebellious sheep get themselves into danger or eaten by wolves, people who make life difficult for the honest priest or pastor trying to look after them are likely to also hurt themselves spiritually.

Good ministers run the risk of being abused by their parishioners (and their bishops!) when they are doing the right thing to look after their flock. So remember that you have a duty to submit and support your pastors to help them carry out their role.

Similarly, they have been charged with a duty to protect you. Here is what the Anglican Prayer Book says in its ordination service that a priest should do:

> YE have heard, Brethren, as well in your private examination, as in the exhortation which was now made to you, and in the holy Lessons taken out of the Gospel, and the writings of the Apostles, of what dignity, and of how great importance this Office is, whereunto ye are called.
>
> And now again we exhort you, in the Name of our Lord Jesus Christ, that ye have in remembrance, into how high a Dignity, and to how weighty an Office and Charge ye are called: that is to say, to be Messengers, Watchmen, and Stewards of the Lord; to teach, and to premonish, to feed and provide for the Lord's family; to seek for Christ's sheep that are dispersed abroad, and for his children who are in the midst of this naughty world, that they may be saved through Christ for ever.
>
> Have always therefore printed in your remembrance, how great a treasure is committed to your charge. For they are the sheep of Christ, which he bought with his death, and for whom he shed his blood. The Church and Congregation whom you must serve, is his Spouse, and his Body. And if it shall happen that the same Church, or any Member thereof, do take any hurt or hindrance by reason of your negligence, ye know the greatness of the fault, and also the horrible punishment that will ensue.
>
> Wherefore consider with yourselves the end of the Ministry towards the children of God, towards the Spouse and Body of Christ; and see that ye never cease your labour, your care and diligence, until ye have done

all that lieth in you, according to your bounden duty, to bring all such as are or shall be committed to your charge, unto that agreement in the faith and knowledge of God, and to that ripeness and perfectness of age in Christ, that there be no place left among you, either for error in religion, or for viciousness in life.

(1662 Book of Common Prayer, Ordering of Priests)

So on one side modern ministers are often too timid about confronting members of their congregation who are behaving badly for fear of personal repercussions. On the other extreme there are ministers who are bullies and control freaks. It is this other extreme that I am warning about. These bullies and control freaks tend to succeed because they are prepared to deal ruthlessly with anyone who opposes them.

Bad leadership can have serious consequences on the church and all those who attend.

CHAPTER TEN

Churches You Should Flee From

Control Cults

The two types of churches I will describe next are not in any sense good. If you find yourself in one I am sure God can tell you when you ask him what you should do. But be prepared that it is likely to be "fight or flight". These sorts of church are generally controlled by fallen human nature (or something worse!). Most likely God will either pull you out to a safer church or ask you to stay as a sort of spiritual secret agent to prepare for his effort to liberate it and bring it again under his rule.

The first of these are control cults.

This is a spiritual problem which usually starts with the minister or stronger power-brokers in the congregation. It can spread to envelop the whole congregation in a dysfunctional co-dependence. It means that fallen human nature has taken over control of the church from the Holy Spirit. You need to be able to recognise it because if you want to keep living to please Jesus you will either get thrown out, have to flee from it or have to fight it.

Don't even think about fighting a control cult without a clear command from God. These people get there by being very good at protecting their position, being very good at grooming church hierarchies to protect them and being very, very ruthless. Often they are supported by evil spiritual powers which are using them to harm Christ's people (although the event that allowed the spiritual powers in may be so long ago and initially such a small step that took the leadership in the wrong direction that they are convinced they are still serving God). So without God's power you stand no chance. With it you may still be a martyr: but in that case God will not let your suffering be in vain.

Here is what Paul said to the Christians of Corinth who had let themselves be spiritually enslaved by some outwardly impressive and fast talking leaders. First this is Paul's evaluation of these particular people:

> For such persons are false apostles, deceitful workers, masquerading as apostles of Christ. And no wonder, for Satan himself masquerades as an angel of light. It is not surprising, then, if his servants also masquerade as servants of righteousness. Their end will be what their actions deserve. (2 Corinthians 11.13-15)

Then he talks about the predisposition of the Corinthian congregation that lets these people lord it over them. "In fact, you even put up with any who enslave you or exploit you or take advantage of you or push themselves forward or slap you in the face." (v.20)

Here is what John said about a church leader a bit like this in the early church:

I wrote to the church, but Diotrephes, who loves to be first, will have nothing to do with us. So when I come, I will call attention to what he is doing, spreading malicious nonsense about us. Not satisfied with that, he refuses to welcome other believers. He also stops those who want to do so and puts them out of the church. (3 John 1.9)

Whether it comes from the minister or whether there is another person in the background pulling the strings or a group of people are controlling the church, they will be exercising the bad kind of authority. They will be dictating to people about things where there should be liberty of conscience. They will be themselves controlled by fallen human nature or worse, and so their dictatorial control will eventually start leading people away from serving God, and to doing things God hates.

Listen to the way people in the church talk. It will give clues about who actually controls the church and what sort of control they exercise. If people are saying "we must obey the minister" too much, that is a warning sign. Another common warning sign is that the church is being run by a faceless leadership. You will hear things like "the leadership says ..." or even worse people saying outright "we must obey the leadership in everything." That all too often means the church is becoming or has become a control cult where a clique has usurped the genuine spiritual authority.

Another bad sign is where honest criticisms or concerns when made to the person in charge of the relevant thing are treated dismissively or worse provoke an outburst of anger or result in some kind of punishment on the person who made them. When making an honest comment, you should expect to be greeted by the fruit of the Spirit: love, patience, charity. If you are met by pride, anger, selfishness, etc., then you need to question how much hold the Holy Spirit really has in their life, regardless of any gifting that might be apparent. (Though keep in mind, you should approach with love, patience and charity, not accusing and stirring up conflict, seeking to serve yourself or demand your "rights".)

A more worrying thing yet is where a church tries to enforce their own ideas regarding issues where Christians should have liberty of conscience. On one hand the example of the minister going round to tell a member of the congregation to stop committing adultery is a good use of authority (though it maybe not be good for the minister when the adulterer complains to the bishop, or stirs up a revolt in the congregation). On the other hand, where the minister or the leadership always want to have their own way or suggests an addition to the Gospel is a matter of salvation, such as doing it 'their way', this is a really bad sign.

I have heard of a case of a congregation in a mainline denomination where the leadership ordered the congregation to shun one family and the congregation blindly obeyed and inflicted this terrible punishment even on the young children. That kind of control cult is really bad. Do not let any minister or any group lead you to do bad things just because they order you to. Remember that you are a morally responsible human being and one day you will have to answer to Jesus for all your actions.

Dead Churches

There are churches where the ministers have not preached the Gospel for years. A common example is where the ministers have been so brainwashed by so called "liberal theology" that all they preach is unbelief.

Sometimes the ministers themselves do truly believe in their hearts, but not in their minds. I have seen 'liberal' ministers who would argue fanatically that the words the Bible says came from Jesus were actually invented by early Christians to meet their own needs and yet these ministers live virtuous lives in obedience to these same commands. On the other side I have seen evangelical ministers who would argue equally fanatically that the whole Bible was the word of God, and yet blatantly disobey some of its commands.

In Matthew 21.28 Jesus told a parable concerning a father and two sons. He asked each to work in his vineyard. The first said "no" but changed his mind and went. The second said "yes" but did not go. Jesus said the first was the one who did what his father wanted. By that the liberal who obeyed the Bible should do better at the Judgement than the evangelical who did not! So remember to discern from their actions, not just their words.

However years of preaching rubbish saps the life of a church, spiritually starves those in the congregation who do really believe, and prevents others from ever hearing enough truth about God to actually become believers. The congregation may be devoted to their priest, they may be very sincere church people, they may be kindly, give generously to the church and charities but they have been deprived of the information about Christ necessary for

Christian growth. So they remain spiritual infants or even just "almost Christians".

If you are socially compatible with the congregation, on joining such a church you could find a very convivial social group. But that is not enough! You need interaction with other grown and growing Christians, including ones who are socially different to you. "The body of Christ" is not a social group. It is precisely a body: lots of different members held together by the head, Jesus. You need people who will encourage, support and pray for you, and keep you accountable for growing in Christ. You need teaching that comes from and is true to the Bible.

Option (1) is to politely leave and find an alive church. Option (2) you should only try if God makes it abundantly clear that this is his purpose for you. It is to stay, gratefully accept the good things this church has to offer, and in return pray for the people and as God gives you opportunity to try to convert and grow them. As Francis Xavier put it, "Always preach the Gospel; if necessary use words."

So keep in mind that some churches will be so infected by heresies that they will either be spiritually dead or taken over by the fruit of human nature: pride, anger, desire for control, etc. Keep in mind that at times these can be quite large or prestigious churches, because they appeal to the flesh or don't preach the difficult teachings of Christ which cause conflict with the world. So don't be deceived by the size or age of a church into thinking they must be safe.

CHAPTER ELEVEN

Ordinary Churches

How To Approach Church

Having said all that, assuming the church you start to go to is a normal, ordinary church my advice is this:

Be prepared to cut them a bit of slack!

This may sound strange but it is applying what the Bible calls "humility" which is a really important and really good attitude, and it is also being kind which is another action the Bible says we should always do.

The people in the church we go to will be sinners like us. They are also (mostly) God's adopted sons and daughters like us. They will still have their annoying sides just as we do. Hopefully they are trying to let God change them day by day into someone that acts like Jesus, just as we are.

So we need a tricky balance of being tolerant of things that we just happen to find annoying or that look a bit silly to us on one hand; and of helping each other to recognise and live up to the behaviour God wants from his children on the other. It is a difficult balance, but at the start it is better to emphasise the "tolerance" bit.

I have pasted below an extract from C. S. Lewis's book *The Screwtape Letters* about what a new convert is likely to think when they first go to church. This is an "opposite sketch" supposedly written from a devil's point of view, but Lewis is using this form to try to say some serious things:

MY DEAR WORMWOOD,

I note with grave displeasure that your patient has become a Christian. Do not indulge the hope that you will escape the usual penalties; indeed, in your better moments, I trust you would hardly even wish to do so. In the meantime we must make the best of the situation. There is no need to despair; hundreds of these adult converts have been reclaimed after a brief sojourn in the Enemy's camp and are now with us. All the habits of the patient, both mental and bodily, are still in our favour.

One of our great allies at present is the Church itself. Do not misunderstand me. I do not mean the Church as we see her spread but through all time and space and rooted in eternity, terrible as an army with banners. That, I confess, is a spectacle which makes our boldest tempters uneasy. But fortunately it is quite invisible to these humans. All your patient sees is the half-finished, sham Gothic erection on the new building estate. When he goes inside, he sees the local grocer with rather an oily expression on his face bustling up to offer him one shiny little book containing a liturgy which neither of them understands, and one shabby little book containing corrupt texts of a number of religious lyrics, mostly bad, and in very small print. When he gets to his pew and looks round him he sees just that selection of his neighbours whom he has hitherto avoided. You want to lean pretty heavily on those neighbours. Make his mind flit to and fro between an expression like "the body of Christ" and the actual faces in the next pew. It matters very little, of course, what kind of people that next pew really contains. You may know one of them to be a great warrior on the Enemy's side. No matter. Your patient, thanks to Our Father below, is a fool. Provided that any of those neighbours sing out of tune, or have boots that squeak, or double chins, or odd clothes, the patient will quite easily believe that their religion must therefore be somehow ridiculous. At his present stage, you see, he has an idea of "Christians" in his mind which he supposes to be spiritual but which, in fact, is largely pictorial. His mind is full of togas and sandals and armour and bare legs and the mere fact that the other people in church wear modern clothes is a real—though of course an unconscious—difficulty to him. Never let it come to the surface; never let him ask what he expected them to look like. Keep everything hazy in his mind now, and you will have all eternity wherein to amuse yourself by producing in him the peculiar kind of clarity which Hell affords.

Work hard, then, on the disappointment or anticlimax which is certainly coming to the patient during his first few weeks as a churchman. The Enemy allows this disappointment to occur on the threshold of every human endeavour. It occurs when the boy who has been enchanted in the nursery by Stories from the Odyssey buckles down to really learning Greek. It occurs when lovers have got married and begin the real task of learning to live together. In every department of life it marks the transition from dreaming aspiration to laborious doing. The Enemy takes this risk because He has a curious fantasy of making all these disgusting little human vermin into what He calls His "free" lovers and servants—"sons" is the word He uses, with His inveterate love of degrading the whole spiritual world by unnatural liaisons with the two-legged animals. Desiring their freedom, He therefore refuses to carry them, by their mere affections and habits, to any of the goals which He sets before them: He leaves them to "do it on their own". And there lies our opportunity. But also, remember, there lies our danger. If once they get through this initial dryness successfully, they become much less dependent on emotion and therefore much harder to tempt.

I have been writing hitherto on the assumption that the people in the next pew afford no rational ground for disappointment. Of course if they do—if the patient knows that the woman with the absurd hat is a fanatical bridge-player or the man with squeaky boots a miser and an extortioner—then your task is so much the easier. All you then have to do is to keep out of his mind the question "If I, being what I am, can consider that I am in some sense a Christian, why should the different vices of those people in the next pew prove that their religion is mere hypocrisy and convention?" You may ask whether it is possible to keep such an obvious thought from occurring even to a human mind. It is, Wormwood, it is! Handle him properly and it simply won't come into his head. He has not been anything like long enough with the Enemy to have any real humility yet. What he says, even on his knees, about his own sinfulness is all parrot talk. At bottom, he still believes he has run up a very favourable credit-balance in the Enemy's ledger by allowing himself to be converted, and thinks that he is showing great humility and condescension in going to church with these "smug", commonplace neighbours at all. Keep him in that state of mind as long as you can.

The Bible puts it this way in Colossians 3.12-14:

Therefore, as God's chosen people, holy and dearly loved, clothe yourselves with compassion, kindness, humility, gentleness and patience. Bear with each other and forgive one another if any of you has a grievance against someone. Forgive as the Lord forgave you. And over all these virtues put on love, which binds them all together in perfect unity.

The other thing we need to extend to our fellow church members is the principle, "In essentials unity; in non-essentials liberty; in all things charity".

So forget that you and they are on opposite sides in politics, or support different football teams. Look at Jesus's disciples: one was a Zealot, the other a tax collector. That is, one had been a resistance fighter trying to kill soldiers of the foreign army controlling their country; the other was an active supporter of this "enemy". They would not have gotten far if they started talking politics to each other (unless of course each of them had left their previous politics behind once they met Jesus). But there they were both members of Jesus's inner twelve.

Forget that they and you have different ideas on any of the many things devout Christians differ on, as the Bible says in Romans 14.1-10:

> Accept those whose faith is weak, without quarrelling over disputable matters. One person's faith allows them to eat everything, but another person, whose faith is weak, eats only vegetables. The one who eats everything must not treat with contempt the one who does not, and the one who does not eat everything must not judge the one who does, for God has accepted that person. Who are you to judge someone else's servant? To their own master they stand or fall. And they will stand, for the Lord is able to make them stand.
>
> Some consider one day more sacred than another; others consider every day alike. Everyone should be fully convinced in their own mind. Those who regard one day as special do so to the Lord. Those who eat meat do so to the Lord, for they give thanks to God; and those who abstain do so to the Lord and give thanks to God. For we do not live to ourselves alone and we do not die to ourselves alone. If we live, we live to the Lord; and if we die, we die to the Lord. So,

whether we live or die, we belong to the Lord. For this very reason, Christ died and returned to life so that he might be the Lord of both the dead and the living.

You, then, why do you judge your brother or sister? Or why do you treat your brother or sister with contempt? For we will all stand before God's judgment seat.

Remember that you cannot always change others, but in any situation with God's help you can change yourself.

PART FIVE

CONCLUSION

Remember Your Foundation

The first step of spiritual survival is to understand exactly what you have been reborn into. This is summarised in the baptismal vows, which are the easy to grasp basics of the Gospel and your salvation. You might not have had a chance to go through baptism classes, or had everything fully explained to you, but now is as good a time as any to start learning. And while you might not be an Anglican by denomination, the 1662 vows are based on the Apostles' Creed, which predates all of the denominations.

The Basics:

- You have changed sides in the war of the universe. You reject the devil, his work and the false worldview he has maintained. You also reject following the desires of your human nature.

- You believe in God: Father, Son and Holy Spirit. You believe in the life, death and resurrection of Jesus, and the judgement at the end of the world, as Christians have throughout history.

- You believe in one Church, which includes all people who have or will ever belong to God.

- And you have sworn to be obedient to God's commands and will for the rest of your life.

Simple.

Once you have accepted that, you are officially "reborn"; born in the spirit instead of the body this time. That's fantastic! Only downside; you are now a baby again, in spiritual terms at least. And as a young Christian, you might not have come across all the problems or diseases that can afflict the spirit. Therefore, you need to protect yourself, and you need to grow! Becoming a Christian is not the end, it is only the beginning of a very long journey.

So, while you are on this earth, you need three things to help you grow and fight the war that is raging. Just for fun, I'm going to present these in a different order to make sure that they have sunken in.

First, all Christians need to pray and develop a life of prayer. Why? Because you have just entered into a relationship with God, and there are no relationships that survive without communication. The act of communicating is what builds and strengths relationships. God is no different. You need to learn how to express what you are feeling and need, as well as over time learning to discern what God might be trying to tell you back. You don't need to hear voices coming from the sky, but do need to trust that God is on the other side of this relationship and might have some opinions on what should be happening.

Second, you need other Christians. The Bible refers to all Christians as a body; all with different parts for different purposes. This suggests that no one can be a Christian by themself. It would be like the hand cutting itself off and hoping to keep on living. You need others, and others need you. They are not going to be perfect, but hey, neither are you. Show God's grace while dealing with others, and as an added bonus this will help you mature much faster than a lot of other things.

Third, once you become a Christian, the battle for your soul really heats up. The devil was basically happy to leave you pretty much alone before, because you were his. Now that you have escaped, you can expect some retaliation. And there is only one way to beat the devil - with the Truth of God. If you don't know your Bible, you are going to be misled someway. It maybe to the right, it maybe to the left, the devil doesn't particularly care. He just wants you to believe lies instead of the truth. Therefore, every believer needs to read and understand their Bible as much as they can.

So what are some of these lies the Devil has been using for centuries?

There are as many heresies as there are people. In one way or another, all of us are heretics in that we believe something that isn't completely true of God, the world or the Bible. However, there are the minor ones which we just need to endure in each other with charity, but then there are more major ones which risk salvation. These you need to stand guard against, defending your baptismal vows with your life.

The first of these types are those that try to add to the Gospel. When it comes to salvation, the Bible has laid out with very strong repetition all that is needed. If anyone tries to make as a matter of salvation something that isn't part of the Gospel, you don't have to stand for that. If they just suggest it is a good idea, well that's one thing. But if they are preaching that all those who do not agree with their additions aren't Christians, then there is a problem. What you were baptised into is what you need to get you into heaven.

The second kind includes those that try to water down the Gospel. While the Gospel is all you need to get into heaven, you need all of it! You can't accept

Jesus, but then reject the parts where he says he is the only way. You don't get to pick and choose from the Bible, or make your relationship with God more convenient by also having relationships with other gods as well. Even if you believe in God, bringing in other practices can be insulting as God has specifically asked us not to.

The third kind of heresy is the garden variety: first used by the serpent in the Garden of Eden. These heresies try to balance out the Gospel with fallen human nature. They want all the benefits of God, with none of the harsh parts. It's like wanting to lose weight, without giving up the chocolate. As it's the weakness of the flesh that has gotten us into this mess in the first place, without dealing with that harshly, we aren't going to be able to obey and follow God. This doesn't mean you need to flog yourself on a daily basis, but you need to understand that sometimes God is going to give you a gift such as healing for his glory, and sometimes he wants to show his glory by giving you strength to overcome your weakness.

You don't need to know every heresy there is in order to protect against them, just as you don't need to drink the entire sea to know that it is salty. A person or church that is in the grip of a heresy will not display the fruit of the Spirit such as love, peace and joy. They will either be filled with the problems of this world: anger, greed, pride, etc., or they will be spiritually dead. They might be very nice people, but have no spark from their connection with God. These are the natural consequences of falling away from the Gospel of salvation. You need God to show you when to stay and try to help, and when to run away screaming. Whichever you do, do it after prayer, consulting the truth of the Bible, and the counsel of godly people.

About The Author

David started his career as a graduate engineer and married Sue, who was studying medicine, then found God had different career goals. So David went to Moore Theological College as an ordination candidate for the Anglican Diocese of Sydney, Australia. He finished off his engineering masters degree thesis in first year college, gained a Th.L. at the end of third year and was expelled for political incorrectness by Sydney theological standards.

Sue said: "OK God, we'll go to the diocese where the Bishop rings us and says, 'Suzie and David, come to my diocese.'" (Which is not how the system works!) A few days later the Bishop of Gippsland rang up ... That year, 1979, David was ordained in Gippsland Anglican Diocese, Victoria.

Sue and David have continued their exciting ride with God ever since. They have run two parishes where large numbers of non-church people have been converted. And they have stayed on long enough to have to confront the problems that follow. Together they have trained up lots of baby Christians as well as their own four delightful children who are all committed Christians.

Recently David semi-retired and started designing and building houses, which Sue happily decorated. But this year he has been called back into the fun of parish life while acting as the locum for Christ Church Anglican Church, St. Kilda. He is also exploring the wide world of blogging, and podcasts his weekly sermons.

For more words of wisdom or adventures in parish life, see Rev. David L. Greentree's website www.LifeUniverseGod.com